In the Name of the People

Pseudo-democracy and the
spoiling of our world

Ivo Mosley

To Helen and

Lo

Ivo.

SOCIETAS
essays in political
& cultural criticism

imprint-academic.com/societas

Published in the UK by
Imprint Academic, PO Box 200, Exeter EX5 5YX, UK

Distributed in the USA by
Ingram Book Company,
One Ingram Blvd., La Vergne, TN 37086, USA

ISBN 9781845402624

A CIP catalogue record for this book is available from the
British Library and US Library of Congress

Contents

The 'sovereign people' is fast becoming a puppet.
— *Herbert Spencer*

Like a rock rolling downhill,
We have reached today.
— *Ishikawa Takuboku*

To destroy a sufficiently deep-seated delusion it is necessary
to show not only its absurdity but also its origins.
— *Lewis Namier*

And then I noticed!
— *David Mercer*, 'For Tea on Sunday'.

One imagines that human nature would rise up incessantly
against despotism: but despite men's love of liberty and hatred
of violence, most peoples are subjected to this type of government. This is easy to understand. In order to form a moderate
government, powers must be knitted together, regulated, tem-
pered and enabled to act; we must give enough ballast, so to
speak, to one power that it can resist others; this is a masterpiece
of legislation that chance rarely produces and that prudence is
rarely allowed to produce. By contrast, a despotic government
jumps into view; it is uniform throughout; only passion is
needed to produce it, and everyone is capable of that.
— *Montesquieu*

Cover design by Andrew Smith:
andy.andrewsmith@hotmail.co.uk

Introduction

A wolf in sheep's clothing is not a sheep: an elected representative claiming to be 'democratic' is not a democrat. Democracy has a simple meaning: 'the people rule'. If the people are not ruling, then the nation is not a democracy. From the standpoint of the people: if we hire someone else to clean our windows, we are not cleaning them ourselves.

Until 1800, everyone knew these simple and obvious truths. Electoral representation was considered to be the very opposite of democracy. If it had to be given a name of Greek origin, the correct one was 'elective oligarchy' meaning 'rule by a few whom we choose to rule us'. As the first chapter of this book relates, it was around the U.S. presidential election of 1800 that candidates first thought of calling themselves 'democrats' to win more votes. After that, it was a question of selling the illusion to all and sundry. A variety of different interest groups — revolutionaries, the new middle class, intellectuals and academics eager for employment — took up the claim, and by about 1920 it was generally accepted: electoral representation *is* democracy. How this happened is the subject of Chapters Two and Three.

The aim of this book is to demonstrate that it is time to dispense with this particular illusion and to introduce some real democracy. Electoral representation is a simple formula by which, in theory, any nation can get a good government. In practice, it is a means by which any nation can get a gigantic bureaucracy, become deeply indebted to a clique of ultra-rich people, and find its assets owned by multinational corporations. There is nothing mysterious or historically odd about this. Representation is a two-way business: representatives negotiate between 'the people' and those in power —

whether that power is a monarch, a military government, a landed aristocracy, political parties or pure money. Representatives are human and do what they have to do, to keep their jobs. This is the subject of Chapters Five and Six.

This is not to say that electoral representation is in itself bad. As an active force, it makes absolutism less likely: the electorate is asked to give some kind of consent, every now and then, to the government it gets. What representation has made possible, however, is bamboozlement on a scale so vast it is impossible to comprehend. Almost the first thing representatives did in England when they became nominally the 'supreme power' (1688) was to make the questionable practices of English bankers legal (this is the subject of Chapter Four). They borrowed money from the same bankers (personally and in the name of 'the people') for their own projects: wars, buying up assets and putting those they dispossessed to profitable work (the profits going to themselves).

The first six chapters of this book are a negative and fragmentary picture of our civilization: a diagnostic report, in the hope that a coroner's report won't be needed soon. The final chapter is an attempt to show that democracy *can* be real and *can* work. Genuinely democratic practices have been included in constitutions in the past and still operate in certain places today. Democracy can be introduced, in its various forms, into our Western systems for the benefit of all, restraining the antics of the powerful and restoring some equity to relations between rich and poor.

Acknowledgements: So many people have helped me that I cannot thank them all; moreover, some insisted on anonymity. I would, however, especially like to thank my family, immediate and extended, for keeping me going; and Keith Sutherland for having what it takes to publish this book.

An apology: substantial changes have been made to parts of this book since review copies were printed and sent out. I apologise to reviewers and readers for any confusion that might arise as a result.

Chapter One

Is 'Democracy' Really Democracy?

There is no greater misnomer in our Western world than calling our systems of electoral representation 'democracies'. This misnomer—or illusion—began to take hold around 1800. Before then 'democracy' was understood to mean the opposite of electoral representation. It meant citizens participating in government in three different ways: by voting directly on issues and appointments; by acting as part-time public officials themselves; and by being members of parliament-type assemblies selected (as juries are) by lot. These practices are all opposite to electoral representation.

Governments formed by election were understood to be not democratic but 'oligarchic'—meaning 'rule by a few' rather than 'rule by the people'. The distinction is obvious and elementary. If we want to rule ourselves, we must be active in ruling, burdensome though that might be. If we choose others to rule us, we no longer rule ourselves: we are not democratic.

Here are some quotes from across the centuries up to 1800 to illustrate how democracy was generally understood. Whether these writers loved democracy or hated it, they did not think that elections were an essential part of the democratic process:

Herodotus (5th Century B.C.):

> Democracy has the fairest of all descriptions—equality in law. Offices are filled by lot, power is held accountable, and all questions are put up for open debate.—from *Histories*, 3.80.6

Plato (428–348 B.C.):

> And democracy comes into power when the poor are the victors, killing some and exiling some, and giving equal shares in the government to all the rest. — from *Republic*, book VIII.

Aristotle (384–322 B.C.):

> It is thought democratic if the offices are assigned by lot; for them to be elected is oligarchic. — from *Politics* IV,1294a.

Cicero (106-43 B.C.):

> Therefore every people, or state, or republic must be ruled by an overall intelligence (consilium) if it is to last. When this is entrusted to one person, we call it monarchy; where it is undertaken by certain select people, we call it aristocracy; when it resides in the people we call it democracy (civitas popularis). — from *The Republic* Book I, 41,42.

Elyot, 1531:

> Another public weal was among the Athenians, where equality was of estate among the people, and only by their whole consent their city and dominions were governed: which might well be called a monster with many heads. Nor never it was certain nor stable; and often times they banished or slew the best citizens, which by their virtue and wisdom had most profited to the public weal. This manner of governance was called in Greek Democratia, in Latin Popularis Potentia, in English the rule of the commonalty. — from *The Book named the Governor*.

Althusius (1557–1638):

> The nature of democracy requires that there be liberty and equality of honours, which consist in these things: that the citizens alternately rule and obey, that there be equal rights for all, and that there be an alteration of private and public life so that all rule in particular matters and individuals obey in all matters. — from *Politica*, 39, 61.

Hobbes (1588–1679):

> The Kinds of Soveraigntie be, as I have now shewn, but three; that is to say, Monarchie, where one Man has it; or Democracie, where the generall Assembly of Subjects hath it; or Aristocracie,

where it is in an Assembly of certain persons nominated, or otherwise distinguished from the rest. —from *Leviathan*.

Montesquieu (1689–1755):

When, in a Republic, the people have the sovereign power, it is a democracy... Selection by lot is natural to democracy; election by choice is natural to aristocracy. —from *De l'Esprit des Lois*, Bk II Ch. 2.

Rousseau (1712–78):

'Selection by lot,' says Montesquieu, 'is democratic in nature.' I agree... But I have already said that real democracy is only an ideal. When election and lot are combined, positions that require special talents, such as military posts, should be filled by the former; the latter is right for cases, such as judicial offices, in which good sense, justice, and integrity are enough, because in a State that is well constituted, these qualities are common to all the citizens. —from *The Social Contract*.

Siéyès (1748-1836):

In democracy, citizens themselves make laws and they nominate directly their public officers. In our plan, the citizens, more or less directly, choose deputies: legislation ceases therefore to be democratic, it becomes representative.

Burke (1729–97):

[describing 'democracy'] Here the people transacted all public business or the greater part of it, in their own persons; their laws were made by themselves and, upon any failure of duty, their officers were accountable to themselves, and to them only. —from *A Letter to Lord ****

Madison (1751–1836):

In a democracy, the people meet and exercise the government in person; in a republic, they assemble and administer it by their representatives and agents. —from *Federalist* 14

From the time of Plato to the time of the French Revolution, historians, politicians and philosophers understood that elections produce oligarchies if the business of government is done in secret, and republics if the business of government is done openly.[1] The story of how elections became 'democratic' in the public mind is so little-known, and so glossed over by most historians and academics, that it is worth retelling in some detail.

The change began in the eighteenth century.[2] Constitutions in Europe at that time were anything but democratic. Monarchs enjoyed power limited by law, custom, and threat of rebellion; and also by institutions such as the church and parliaments. Some portions of these parliaments—for instance the House of Commons in England—were elected. Jurists began to refer to these elected assemblies (though the vote was restricted to males with property) as the 'democratical element' in the otherwise undemocratic constitutions of their day. For instance, in his 1762 lectures on jurisprudence Adam Smith wrote that there were no 'true democracies of the ancient type' in the Europe of his day; but that within monarchical systems, electoral representation was a 'democraticall element'. Blackstone, in his *Commentary* of 1765, wrote: 'with regard to the elections of knights, citizens, and burgesses; we may observe that herein consists the exercise of the democratical part of our constitution.'

These are the beginnings of the modern tradition, of regarding representation as a 'democratic' procedure. The Marquis d'Argenson is credited with the first written assertion (1764) that 'democratical elements' could constitute 'a democracy' in their own right. In addition, he maintained

---

[1]   In an interesting exception to this generality, Aquinas equates democracy with 'the people having the right to choose their rulers' and attributes this to Divine law as made manifest in Deutoronomy 1. It is an example of a thread in our political traditions (others are kingship, divine sanction and suffrage) which derives from Biblical rather than Graeco-Roman or Germanic traditions. This is a theme somewhat underexplored in the literature. (*Summa Theologica*, I-II, Question 105, Answer 1.)

[2]   The following are are some surveys of usage of the word 'democracy' in early modern times: Charles A. Beard,*The Republic* (1943), pp. 27ff.; in R.R. Palmer, *The Age of the Democratic Revolution* (1959), pp. 13-19, and 'Notes on the Use of the Word "Democracy" 1789-1799', *Political Science Quarterly*, June 1953; Pierre Rosanvallon, 'L'histoire du mot democratie dans l'epoque moderne' in *Le Situation de la démocratie* (1993).

that the kind of 'democracy' provided by representation was truer and better than the 'false' democracy of the ancients:

> False democracy falls soon to anarchy: it is the government of the multitude, of a people in revolt and therefore insolent, scorning both law and reason; its tyrannical despotism is recognised in the violence of its actions and the waywardness of its deliberations. In true democracy, people act through deputies and these deputies are authorised by election. The mission of those elected by the people, and the authority resting on them, constitute public power: their duty is to stipulate for the interests of the greatest number of citizens, to save them from evils and to procure them goods.[3]

This idea of the Marquis seems to have been ignored by writers of his own generation, but it was taken up at an ominous and significant moment—5th February 1794—in a speech by the revolutionary Robespierre. He combined it with some resonant language taken from Montesquieu, to justify the first large-scale 'democratic' terror of the modern age:

> Democracy is not a state in which the people, continually assembled, itself directs public affairs; still less is it a state in which a hundred thousand fragments of the people, by contradictory, hasty and isolated measures, should decide on the destiny of society as a whole; such a government has never existed and if it did, it could do nothing but throw the people back into despotism...
>
> Democracy is a state in which the people, as sovereign, guided by laws of its own making, does for itself all that it can do well, and by its delegates what it cannot...[4] But, to establish and consolidate democracy among us, it is necessary to bring the war of

---

[3] From Considérations Sur le Government Ancien et Present de la France, Chapter One.

[4] An almost verbatim quote from Montesquieu, *De LEsprit des Lois* 'bk. 2 ch.2, except that he changes Montesquieu's 'ministers' to 'delegates' and misses out Montesquieu's 'fundamental maxim' that in a democracy ministers should be named by the people—not rise to power by sinister manipulation as did Robespierre.

liberty against tyranny to a conclusion… such is the aim of the emergency regime.[5]

These words were spoken to the National Convention. Robespierre was taking upon himself the management of the revolution, organising genocide in the Vendée and mass murder throughout France. Here, at the very origin of 'representative democracy' we see a phenomenon that would become familiar: a 'leader' claiming to represent the people, abusing his claim in the most extreme way.[6]

Selection by lot to form assemblies—the second characteristic of 'ancient' true democracy—was never considered as a form of government by the English, American or French revolutionaries, despite the fact that some of their favourite philosophers—Rousseau, Harrington and Montesquieu—considered lot to be the essence of democracy.[7] Several reasons have been suggested for this neglect. First, lot was considered impracticable, given the difficulties of travel and communication;[8] second, it was considered undesirable, given the lack of education and understanding in many citizens;[9] third, having fought so hard for power, revolutionaries were not about to hand it over to others.[10]

---

[5]   Quoted by R.R. Palmer, *Political Science Quarterly*, June 1953.

[6]   The relationship between democracy and genocide is explored in *The Dark Side of Democracy* (Mann) and *The Meaning of Genocide* (Levene).

[7]   See Bernard Manin, *The Principles of Representative Government* (1997). Lot was, however, introduced in France for jury service (1790) and later to select soldiers for conscription (1818).

[8]   'In the modern republicks every person is free, and the poorer sort are all employed in some necessary occupation. They would therefore find it a very great inconvenience to be obliged to assemble together and debate concerning public affairs or trials of causes'—Adam Smith, *Lectures on Jurisprudence* (Liberty Fund Edition p. 226).

[9]   Roger Sherman at the Constitutional Convention: 'The people should have as little to do as may be about the government. They lack information and are constantly liable to be misled.'

[10]   An example of this is the manipulated franchise for Cromwell's Parliaments after the English Civil War: unless a man could provide evidence that he had supported the winning side, he was not allowed to vote. See Little and Smith, *Parliaments and Politics during the Cromwellian Protectorate*, p. 51; Gardiner, *Constitutional Documents*, pp. 363-4.

In America, the Founding Fathers did not use the word 'democracy' in its new sense: they used it in the old-fashioned way, meaning citizen assemblies and selection by lot. They disapproved of it mightily. Their remarks are illuminating:

> Democracies have ever been spectacles of turbulence and contention... and have in general been as short in their lives as they have been violent in their deaths. (Madison, 1787)

> The ancient democracies, in which the people themselves deliberated, never possessed one feature of good government. Their very nature was tyranny. (Hamilton, 1787)

> Democracy wastes, exhausts, and murders itself. There was never a democracy that did not commit suicide. (John Adams, 1814)

> Democracy is impracticable beyond the limits of a town. (Jefferson, 1816)

Benjamin Franklin (1706-90) is credited (perhaps wrongly, though it's not out of character) with the statement: 'Democracy is two wolves and a sheep voting on what's for dinner.'

The system the founding fathers wanted was republican and unashamedly based on 'rule by the few'. Jefferson wrote that power should be entrusted to a 'natural aristocracy' of the most talented and virtuous, replacing the old 'artificial aristocracy founded on wealth and birth'. Elections would give people the right to choose those 'natural aristocrats'. In Madison's words, public opinion would be 'refined and enlarged' by passing it 'through the medium of a chosen body of citizens, whose wisdom may best discern the true interest of their country.'

The first setback in the idea of the people choosing a new 'natural aristocracy' was the development of the political party. How were voters to know enough about an individual standing for election to judge whether or not they were a 'natural aristocrat'? Unless the candidate were a near neighbour, it was impossible. Political parties appeared not only as the judge of who was a 'natural aristocrat' but also as a rough indication as to the opinions of a candidate. From there it was an extremely short step to the system we are familiar with today: the party chooses obedient and faithful servants, the kind of people who will tailor their opinions, principles and actions to the demands of party 'wire-pullers' (the old-fashioned word for puppet-masters). The system was trumped at the outset, and the founding fathers knew it. Most of their later regrets, privately expressed, were along these lines.

As for democracy: for the founding fathers, the word 'democrat' was an insult. Washington wrote to his friend James McHenry in 1798 (the language is that of a slave-owner): 'you could as soon scrub a blackamoor white as change the principles of a profest democrat; and that he will leave nothing unattempted to overturn the government of this country'.

The event during which a proportion of ordinary Americans began to think of themselves as 'democrats' was the protracted presidential election of 1800.

The votes of the people had been cast. The Electoral College and the House of Representatives were in deadlock over who should be inaugurated president. Rival state militias (Virginia and Pennsylvania vs. Massachusetts) were ready to march on Washington to take control of the government. Jefferson, the Republican candidate, had the largest share of the popular vote (ironically, this included votes of slaves appropriated by their masters at three-fifths of a vote for each slave owned). Jefferson's supporters claimed that the will of the numerical majority should prevail.[11] Jefferson became president, and civil war was averted.

During the crisis, it had become apparent that there was a strong demand among Americans for 'democracy' not as a political system but as a feeling that 'the people' should be in

---

[11] Although he would not embrace the term 'democrat', Jefferson praised the principle of majority rule in his inaugural speech: 'Absolute acquiescence in the decisions of the majority [is] the vital principle of republics, from which there is no appeal but to force, [which is] the vital principle and immediate parent of despotism.' See Charles A. Beard, *The Republic*, p. 53.

charge of their own destiny. Only the most educated among them knew that democracy had a tradition of its own in direct opposition to electoral representation. The majority of new 'democrats' looked to elections to satisfy the democratic impulse. Representatives, in their view, should be delegates of the popular will rather than 'a natural aristocracy of talent'.

Jefferson himself preferred a 'natural aristocracy' but he kept quiet about it in public and allowed himself to be carried to power in the name of democracy. He referred to his victory as 'the revolution of 1800'. 'The nation declared its will,' he wrote, 'by dismissing functionaries of one principle and electing those of another'. The new 'democratic'[12] principle was made official, as Jefferson's party changed its name, piecemeal and via local party organisations over the next twenty years, from 'Republican' to 'Democratic-Republican'. In 1809, the popular writer Elias Smith proclaimed: 'My friends, let us *never* be ashamed of democracy!'

To some observers, however, the change was not from 'natural aristocracy' to democracy, but from good aristocracy to bad aristocracy: in other words, a classic Aristotelian switch from aristocracy to oligarchy.[13] John Tazewell wrote in 1804: 'How fast is this government of ours settling into aristocracy; and aristocracy of the worst kind, the aristocracy supported by intrigue.'[14] The intrigue that Tazewell (and many others) complained about was the misuse of Congress for the pursuit of business interests.

This misuse, however, was a corruption waiting to happen. Madison had already proposed (1787) in *The Federalist*

---

[12] Jefferson himself was aware of the difference between electoral representation and democracy, and he continued to refer to his party as 'Republican'. He reserved the word democracy for use in its old sense—as in his quote above, from 1816.

[13] Aristotle held that every form of government—rule by one, by a few, or by the *demos*, could exist in a good or bad form depending upon whether it ruled selfishly or in the interests of everyone. Aristocracy was 'good rule by a few'; oligarchy was 'bad rule by a few'.

[14] 21 April 1804, *Tazewell Papers*, Va. State Library, quoted in Fischer, *The Revolution of American Conservatism*, Harper & Rowe (1969), p. 32.

that the main business of Congress should be a regulation of interests (the interests of the poor, however, who make up Aristotle's *demos* are not mentioned):

> A landed interest, a manufacturing interest, a mercantile interest, a moneyed interest, with many lesser interests, grow up of necessity in civilised nations, and divide them into different classes, actuated by different sentiments and views. The regulation of these various and interfering interests forms the principal task of modern legislation, and involves the spirit of party and faction in the necessary and ordinary operations of the government.[15]

Business interests were the basis of alliances in political parties which quickly came to dominate political life, much to the disgust of many who had fought for the revolution. Washington made this the central theme of his Farewell Address:

> They [political parties] serve to organize faction, to give it an artificial and extraordinary force; to put, in the place of the delegated will of the nation, the will of a party, often a small but artful and enterprising minority of the community; and, according to the alternate triumphs of different parties, to make the public administration the mirror of the ill-concerted and incongruous projects of faction, rather than the organ of consistent and wholesome plans digested by common counsels, and modified by mutual interests. However combinations or associations of the above description may now and then answer popular ends, they are likely, in the course of time and things, to become potent engines, by which cunning, ambitious, and unprincipled men will be enabled to subvert the power of the people, and to usurp for themselves the reins of government.[16]

Washington immortalised his objection to populist vote-mongering in a single pithy sentence:

---

[15] The Federalist, Number Ten. It is quoted by Charles Beard in *An Economic Interpretation of the Constitution of the United States* (1913).

[16] Washington's Farewell Address, paragraphs 17, 18.

> That party could set up a broomstick, call it a true son of liberty
> and a democrat, and it would command their votes *in toto*.[17]

The rise to power and influence of political parties meant
that from then on, prospective representatives would be
chosen by secretive power structures remote from the lives
of ordinary people. Candidates for office would depend on
powerful commercial interests even before they began to
canvas votes. The idea of a 'natural aristocracy of talent' became a little boat adrift in a sea of sharks.

Parties who get together to 'regulate' their 'various and
interfering interests' can hardly be expected to refrain from
making deals and divvying up spoils, let alone from agree-
ing on preferential treatments which benefit all business at
the expense of the rest. It is the very nature of business to
identify opportunities and exploit them.[18] Congress became,
and has remained, a forum for the interests and advance-
ment of business. The dominant ethic and the creed of
power in America is that the interests of business *are* the interests of the nation.

The implications of party politics for 'democratic representation' are fairly obvious: representatives are no longer
representatives of the people, but negotiators with the people on behalf of the powers that secure their employment.
Voters, of course, are not *obliged* to vote for party candidates:
if they wish, they can vote for independents. However, with
the odd exception, it is impracticable for voters to make an
informed choice about who they might want to vote for
unless candidates carry the stamp of party identification.

---

[17]   Letter to Jonathan Trumbull, 21/07/99.
[18]   Adam Smith: 'The proposal of any new law or regulation of commerce
which comes from this order [*i.e. from those who live by profit*], ought always to be listened to with great precaution, and ought never to be
adopted till after having been long and carefully examined, not only
with the most scrupulous, but with the most suspicious attention. It
comes from an order of men, whose interest is never exactly the same
with that of the public, who have generally an interest to deceive and
even to oppress the public, and who accordingly have, upon many occa-
sions, both deceived and oppressed it.' From *The Wealth of Nations*, Book
1, Chapter 11.

Most voters today imagine that choosing between political parties is what democracy *is*. Perhaps this illusion has been a good thing for the last two hundred years: it allowed a relatively smooth transition from aristocratic and monarchic rule. However, it has created a brand-new machinery of power and a new elite that is anything but 'democratic'.

The next chapter is the story of how representative government became accepted in Europe as the best—or least worst—alternative among possible forms of government; how it was (to begin with at least) effectively rule by the middle class; and how it came to be called *democracy*.

a less antiquated way; perhaps even by themselves, according to principles of 'reason, truth and justice'.[1]

Reason, truth and justice, however, cannot be implemented without institutions and authority of government. The myth of 'representative democracy' arose out of the practical need of the middle classes to sanction their rule and give moral authority to their administration of society. The illusion that electing representatives is 'democratic' was fostered by apologists for middle-class rule during times when very few of 'the people' were even allowed to vote. One by one, these countries came to call their systems 'democratic'.

In Britain, belief in 'representative democracy' took over without much opposition. John Millar, a pupil of Adam Smith, wrote straightforwardly in 1803 that electoral representation was 'democracy for the modern age'.[2] John Stuart Mill, the most celebrated theorist of liberal middle-class rule, worked hard to justify this belief—with certain logical contortions, as we shall see. At the more radical end of the spectrum, agitators did not call for any kind of popular participation in government: they either took democracy to mean 'votes for all' or they called for socialism.[3] Only a few dissenting voices protested that there was a logical contradiction inherent in 'representative democracy'.[4]

In America, as we saw in Chapter One, the doctrine that representation could be democratic was born among a vocal minority around 1800. It became further established in the 1820's as Andrew Jackson tried to extend the voting franchise to all adult white males: he called this process 'democratization'. Over the next eighty years, Americans gradually

---

[1] Guizot's phrase, elaborated in *The Origins of Representative Government*.

[2] *An Historical View of the English Government*, Section 3, pp. 325/6. Republished by Liberty Fund, 2006.

[3] Radical agitators have never shown much inclination to hand over power to those they represent: like other professional representatives, they want to keep it to themselves.

[4] For instance, G.C. Lewis in *Remarks on the Use and Abuse of Some Political Terms* (1832); John Austin in *A Plea for the Constitution* (1859); Henry Maine in *Popular Government* (1885). Lewis was expected to be leader of the Liberal Party before his sudden death in 1863.

Chapter Two

'Representative Democracy': Establishing the Illusion

Chapter One showed that electoral representation wasn't thought of as democratic until around the year 1800, and that until then it was thought of as the opposite of democracy—as 'rule by the few', or oligarchy. The logic behind the older opinion is simple and obvious. Democracy means 'rule by the people' and electing representatives is choosing others to rule for you. This chapter is about how the illusion of 'representative democracy' became established during the nineteenth and early twentieth centuries in Britain and Europe.

That authority and power should rest upon an illusion is nothing new. For at least a thousand years in Europe—say, between the coronation of Pippin the Short and the decapitation of Louis XVI—authoritative rule was based on the illusion that kingship conferred magical, even divine qualities upon its possessor. By 1800, this illusion had worn more than a little thin. Power and property were increasingly in the hands of a new wealthy middle class, many of whom were convinced that government could be better managed in came to think of their system and their nation as 'democratic': according to historian Charles Beard, the process was complete by the time of the First World War.[5]

From early in the nineteenth century, Europeans were inclined to regard America as a test case for democracy. In the words of John Stuart Mill:

> America is usually cited by the two great parties which divide Europe, as an argument for or against democracy. Democrats have sought to prove by it that we ought to be democrats; aristocrats, that we should cleave to aristocracy, and withstand the democratic spirit.[6]

Only in France was there substantial resistance among the middle classes to the idea that representative government was 'democratic', and this makes the story of its acceptance in France particularly interesting. As we saw in Chapter One, Robespierre was an early advocate of 'representative democracy', saying quite straightforwardly that democracy meant people handing over power and sovereignty to representatives. In the context of the Terror, which he was then directing into its most murderous phase, the argument was about who was entitled to kill without due process of law. A previous set of massacres (in September 1792) had been carried out by people's assemblies — in other words, by ancient democratic methods.[7] In his speech of February 5th 1794, Robespierre asserted that the right to commit murder belonged only to political representatives. 'The Revolution owes only death to the enemies of the people.'[8]

---

[5]   *The Republic* (1943), pp. 32-3.

[6]   His first review of *Democracy in America* (1835).

[7]   There is longstanding disagreement about this, mostly on ideological grounds. Is 'le peuple' capable of spontaneous massacre? See Acton, *Lectures on the French Revolution*, Liberty Fund edition, p. 211*ff.*

[8]   In this way, Robespierre's 'representative democracy' established the right of representatives not just to create law but also, in their executive capacity, to break it in the name of the people, a right which has dogged representative democracy ever since. The danger is theoretically less where the executive and legislature are separate; but in the USA, George W. Bush established the right of the president to order assassinations.

Thirty years later, after the expulsion of Napoleon (1815), Robespierre's Terror was still a living memory. Many citizens had lost close relations, and had perhaps only survived themselves by the skin of their teeth. The word 'democracy' had become associated with two sets of murders: 'ancient democracy' with massacres organised by popular assemblies, 'new democracy' with murders organised by representatives.[9] To complicate matters further, Rousseau, the most influential thinker among progressives, was dismissive of democracy and had nothing but contempt for representation: 'the moment a people allows itself to be represented,' he said, 'it is no longer free: it no longer exists.'[10]

After Napoleon's expulsion, an exhausted France looked to the past for institutions which might bring stability to government. Louis XVIII[11] was summoned as King, and a representative government was set up on principles approximating those of English constitutional monarchy. Voting rights were based on property; the legislature was elected; executive ministers were nominated by the King after consultation with the legislature. In this way, representatives were once again making laws: and once again, there was separation between them and the executive power.

The great advantage of this was that power was not all in the hands of one cabal. But it was still in the hands of one class. Voting was restricted to males with property. The executive was chosen with the approval of the legislature, so

---

9   The association was all the worse as Robespierre came to power during the only attempt at 'universal suffrage' made during the Revolution. See P. Guéniffey, *Le Nombre et La Raison* (1993). ('Universal suffrage' meant adult male, excluding servants and those with no permanent address. Elections were indirect, and representatives had to be propertied.)

10 Rousseau, *The Social Contract*. Book III, Chapter 15. On democracy: 'Were there a people of gods, their government would be democratic. A government so perfect is not suited to men.' The question has often been asked: of what sort of government did Rousseau actually approve? The answer seems to be, a sovereignty of laws made directly by all citizens, directed by a spirit of loyalty to the public good; the executive to consist of magistrates guided by these laws.

11 Brother of the decapitated Louis XVI. (Louis XVII, son and heir to Louis XVI, had been murdered as a child in prison.)

that too represented middle-class interests. It was self-evidently rule by the middle class: no one tried to deny that fact, or to give it the name 'democracy'.

In these circumstances, the word 'democracy' lost its association with massacre and came to mean pressure from below — from the poor — to gain influence and power in politics.[12] It was often associated with images of water, of rivers flooding their banks. For instance the Comte de Serre, addressing Parliament in 1822, spoke of the 'torrent' of democracy 'threatening to overflow the feeble banks that barely contain it.'[13] Democracy' became an emotive word: for the rich it was a bogey-monster, and for the radical poor it was a rallying-call.

The distinction between representative government and democracy was emphasized by Guizot — later to become prime minister of France — in a series of lectures which made him famous.[14] 'Starting from the principle that truth, reason and justice — in a word, divine law — alone possess rightful power,' he wrote, 'representative government... is a method of collecting into one focus, and of realizing, public reason and public morality, and of calling them to the occupation of power'. He dismissed democracy as 'despotism and privilege in the hands of the majority'.

As prime minister, Guizot and his fellow-ministers acted 'as if the intelligent middle class was destined by Heaven to govern.'[15] This conviction was based on several self-evident facts. First, 'representative' and 'bureaucrat' are middle-class occupations. Second, the qualities needed for responsible rule are middle-class: education, aptitude for organisation, and vocational integrity. Thirdly, the other two classes had

---

[12] For these paragraphs I am indebted to accounts by R.R. Palmer, 'Notes on the Use of the Word 'Democracy' 1789-99' in *Political Science Quarterly*, 1953, and Pierre Rosanvallon, 'The History of the Word "Democracy" in France', *Journal of Democracy*, 1995.

[13] Quoted in Rosanvallon, op. cit.

[14] These lectures, given in 1821/22, were later published in English translation as *The History of the Origins of Representative Government*. See in particular Part Two, Lecture 10.

[15] Lord Acton, *The History of Freedom and Other Essays* (1922) p. 92.

disgraced themselves historically: the upper classes during the violent oppressions of feudalism and absolute monarchy, the lower classes during the murderous excesses of revolution. 'Above the middle class,' wrote Royer Collard 'is a lust for power; below it there is ignorance, the habit of dependence and therefore the incapacity of exercising the functions in question.'[16]

These middle-class liberals did not want to give votes to the poor, whose ignorance and desperate condition made them prey to extremists: 'the instrument of intrigue and passion'[17] to be played upon by both absolute monarchists and 'idolaters of democracy'.[18]

Thus, representative government in France was founded in opposition to democracy. France was out of step with Britain and America, where it was already common opinion that representation was democratic: but not for long. The same fear which prompted the illusion of 'representative democracy' in Britain and America was active in France: the masses were still excluded from government, despite all the political upheavals of Revolution, dictatorship and restoration.[20] It took a work of near-genius to bring France in line with Britain and America, and that work was *Democracy in America* by Alexis de Tocqueville — published in two parts (1835 and 1840).

Initially, Tocqueville's use of the word 'democracy' was strictly in line with his French contemporaries:

> Democracy! Don't you notice that these are the waters of the flood? ... Already they cover the fields and the cities; they roll over the destroyed battlements of fortified castles and come to wash against the steps of thrones. ... So let us know how to face the future steadily and with open eyes. Instead of wanting to

---

16   Royer Collard, quoted in *Cambridge Modern History* (1934), X, p 52.
17   Barante, quoted in *Cambridge Modern History* (1934), X, p. 51.
18   Guizot's phrase in *Democracy in France* (1848).
20   In some ways they were more oppressed under middle class rule than they had been under the old regime: for instance, the Le Chapelier law, forbidding workers' associations, was passed in 1791 and not repealed until 1884.

raise impotent dikes, let us build the holy, tutelary ark which must carry the human species over this ocean without shores.[21]

His great fear was that this flood from below would produce a despot, as it had done repeatedly during the Revolution:

> To claim to stop the march of democracy would be folly. God willing, there is still time to direct it and to prevent it from leading us to the despotism of one man, that is to say the most detestable form of government that the human mind has ever been able to imagine.[22]

Unless it was managed properly, democracy would gobble up the upper classes just as it had gobbled up monarchies:

> Do you think that, having destroyed feudalism and vanquished kings, democracy will retreat before the bourgeois and the rich? Will it stop now that it has become so strong and its adversaries so weak?[23]

Tocqueville travelled to America to understand how popular government worked there, to advise how it could be managed safely and satisfactorily back at home.[24] He wanted to 'point out, if possible, how to escape tyranny and debasement while becoming *democratic*'.[25] 'The entire book you are about to read,' wrote Tocqueville, 'has been written under the impression of a sort of religious terror.'

> To instruct democracy, to re-animate if possible its beliefs, to purify its mores… such is the first of duties imposed today on those who lead society.[26]

Tocqueville was impressed by the political stability he found in America. During his lifetime, France was racked

---

[21]   Nolla edition p. 12.
[22]   Nolla edition p. 13. Before Tocqueville died 'democracy' had indeed led to despotism (Napoleon III).
[23]   Nolla edition p. 14.
[24]   'Though I seldom mentioned France, I wrote not a page without thinking of her.' Letter, 19th Oct 1843.
[25]   Tocqueville's italics. Quoted in Nolla edition, p. 32.
[26]   Nolla edition, p. 16.

with revolutions, wars and social upheaval. As well as the revolutions of 1789, 1830 and 1848 there were the Napoleonic wars, a restoration of the monarchy, two forced abdications, a short-lived presidential system, a *coup d'état* (1851) and the beginning of a short-lived empire under Louis-Napoleon. In contrast to this turmoil, America was relatively constant. 'While all the nations of Europe were ravaged by war or torn apart by civil discords,' Tocqueville wrote later, 'the American people alone in the civilized world remained at peace.'[27] From this came his determination to rehabilitate 'democracy'—in its American manifestation—in his native France.

Tocqueville's book was a wild and immediate success both at home and abroad. It reassured Frenchmen that, cloaked in a guise of democracy, representation could be managed by the middle classes.

Attempting to reconcile his knowledge of history with his claim that representation is democratic, Tocqueville—a highly educated, phenomenally gifted and compulsively honest individual—redefined 'democracy' in so many different ways that it has become almost a game to identify them: by the time he pulled the final rabbit out of the hat, even he was puzzled. Democracy was 'the flood from below'; it was 'middle-class government'; it was 'self-government'; finally he settled on 'equality of social condition'.[28]

'Equality of social condition', according to Tocqueville, meant not so much equality of wealth, or even of opportunity, as a complete rejection of the hierarchy of privileges and esteems that had characterised European societies for over a thousand years. Citizens in America, according to Tocqueville, regarded and treated each other as social equals, no matter how different they were in wealth or im-

---

[27] From the introduction to the twelfth edition of *Democracy in America*.
[28] Pierson (1959), Lively (1962), Zetterbaum 1967), Schleifer (2000) and Craiatu (2003) have all devoted chapters to what Tocqueville meant by 'democracy'.

portance.[29] It is hard for us now to imagine how novel this must have appeared to a nineteenth-century European, accustomed to not just overt deference from lower to higher classes, but also to easy identification of who belonged to which class through dress, speech and manners.

'Equality of social condition', Tocqueville wrote, is 'the primary fact of democracy' which 'extends its influence far beyond political customs and laws... it creates opinions, gives birth to sentiments, suggests customs and modifies all that it does not produce.' That this 'equality' was merely an equality of manners seemed not to bother Tocqueville. Ignoring manifest inequalities such as slavery, powerful secret societies, plutocratic law-making and great inequalities of wealth, he claimed that American 'democracy' gave sovereignty to of all the people.

> I know of only two ways to make equality reign in the political world. Rights must be given to each citizen or to no one. For peoples who have come to the same social state as the Anglo-Americans, it is very difficult to envisage a middle course between the sovereignty of all and the absolute sovereignty of one.[30]

By 'sovereignty of all' Tocqueville did not mean that all would actually participate:

> The most rational government is not the one in which *all* those interested take part, but the one that the most enlightened and the most moral classes of society lead.[31]

The people are sovereign whether laws are made 'by the people in a body' or 'by its representatives, chosen by universal suffrage.'[32] Tocqueville's apotheosis of democracy as popular sovereignty is mystical, almost ecstatic:

---

[29] *Democracy in America,* Introductory chapter.
[30] Part One, Chapter 3. See Pierre Manent, *Tocqueville and the Nature of Democracy,* (1996), pp.2ff.
[31] Letter to Kergolay (1831), quoted in Nolla, p. 317.
[32] Nolla, p. 97.

The People rules the American political world as God rules the universe. It is the cause and the end of all things. Everything arises out of it and all is absorbed by it.[33]

The one meaning he specifically denies democracy is its ancient one of participation. He dismisses the ancient democracies as a sham, and utterly dissimilar from what he was talking about:

I am not afraid to declare that those pretended democracies were made up of elements very different from ours, and that they had nothing in common with ours but the name.[34]

Tocqueville's distinction is confused and hard to justify, considering he himself locates the origins of American democracy in the townships of New England, whose governance was along the lines of 'old' democracy: laws were decided by the whole people, magistrates were selected by lot and by rota, election was limited to choosing 'selectmen' for specialist administrative positions. Tocqueville's dismissal of old 'pretended' democracy appears somewhat forced and anxious, as if he is determined to obliterate it as a rival.[35]

Reactions to Tocqueville's book were mostly ecstatic. John Stuart Mill, for instance:

It has at once taken its place among the most remarkable productions of our time ... M. de Tocqueville's is, in our eyes, the true view of the position in which mankind now stands. ... We have it not in our power to choose between democracy and aristocracy; necessity and Providence have decided that for us. But the choice we are still called upon to make is between a well and an ill-regulated democracy; and on that depends the future well-being of the human race.[36]

Guizot was more critical. Referring to Tocqueville's aristocratic contempt for the bourgeoisie, and to his belief that

---

[33]   Book One, Chapter 4. Nolla, p. 97. This sentence is curiously omitted in some editions.

[34]   Book Three, Chapter 15.

[35]   He was equally rude about traditional democracy in his speech on democracy in Switzerland, where direct and participatory forms of democracy still survived (and still survive).

[36]   *London Review* (October 1835).

out of the working class might come some form of greatness, Guizot wrote in a letter: 'You judge democracy like a vanquished aristocrat who is convinced his conqueror must be right.'[37]

Following the populist and socialist revolutions of 1848, the middle classes propagated the myth of representative democracy with new urgency. Communists and socialists had shown they had enough popular support to replace existing elites, if only temporarily, with their own personnel. After brutally suppressing the revolutions of 1848 the old orders of Europe, including the government of France, granted extensions of suffrage to the ordinary working man — loudly calling these extensions 'democracy'.[38]

Sceptics of the new 'democracy' returned to using the word in an older sense, meaning the desires and efforts of the masses for a genuine share in government.[39] Guizot dismissed arguments about whether democracy is inherently 'good' or 'bad' and reminded us that democratic pressure can (like most forces) be used for either:

> Democracy springs from the struggle between good and evil, which is the main fact of our nature and of our condition in the world. It is the war-cry, the battle standard, of the many below against the few above; sometimes raised in the name of the most sacred rights, sometimes in the name of the grossest, most senseless passions; sometimes against the most iniquitous usurpations, sometimes against the most legitimate powers.[40]

Most writers after Tocqueville, however, simply devoted themselves to reinforcing the new myth: 'the people' can only take charge of their own destiny in the modern world

---

[37] Quoted by Craiutu in Liberalism under Siege: The Political Thought of the French Doctrinaires (2003) p.92.

[38] Acton writing in 1878: 'Scarcely thirty years separate the Europe of Guizot and Metternich from these days of universal suffrage both in France and in Germany.' (The opening words of his essay 'Sir Erskine May's Democracy in Europe'.)

[39] As well as Guizot, see Acton op.cit. and Dicey, Law and Opinion in England (1914), pp. 48 ff.

[40] 'De la démocratie dans les sociétés modernes', 1838. My translation.

by electing representatives, and the resulting government is inherently good.

It came as a shock when the sociologist Robert Michels, in a book published in 1911, revealed that representatives of the people, even socialists and communists, were by-and-large solidly middle-class in origin as well as occupation. Was it meaningful to call a system 'democratic' in which all rulers and would-be rulers were middle class?[41] By that time, however, the democratic myth reigned supreme: no sudden flash of reason was going to hold it back. Michels' book was only a temporary embarrassment.

More recently, electoral representation has been applauded by some writers as perhaps not exactly *democracy*, but actually a better form of government than true democracy, combining the three classic forms (monarchy, aristocracy and democracy) in one do-it-all product.[42] Presidents are the monarchical element, legislatures the aristocratic and voting the democratic element.[43] This would be more plausible if the 'democratic' element had more substance and if representatives were independent of party puppet-masters.

According to historian Charles Beard, electoral representation was finally accepted as a form of 'democracy' around the time of the First World War.

> Nothing like official sanction was given to the idea that the United States is first and foremost a democracy until Woodrow Wilson, in making the war against the Central Powers a war for democracy, gave the stamp of wide popularity to the idea that the United States is, first and foremost, a democracy.[45]

---

41 Political Parties: A Sociological Study of the Oligarchical Tendencies of Modern Democracy.

42 For instance Bernard Manin, in his (otherwise) excellent book *The Principles of Representative Government* (1997).

43 M.H. Hansen, the leading historian of ancient Greek democracy, argues that modern presidents have more kingly power than their early-modern monarchical predecessors ('The mixed constitution versus the separation of powers: Monarchical and aristocratic aspects of modern democracy', *History of Political Thought*, XXXI, 2010, pp. 509-531.)

45 *The Republic*, p. 32.

The story preceding Wilson's 'war for democracy' is as significant as any in the history of our myth. In 1912, Woodrow Wilson wrote in *The New Freeedom*:[46]

> Suppose you go to Washington and try to get at your government. You will always find that while you are politely listened to, the men really consulted are the men who have the biggest stake—the big bankers, the big manufacturers, the big masters of commerce, the heads of railroad corporations and of steamship corporations. I have no objection to these men being consulted, because they also, though they do not themselves seem to admit it, are part of the people of the United States. But I do very seriously object to these gentlemen being *chiefly* consulted, and particularly to their being exclusively consulted, for, if the government of the United States is to do the right thing by the people of the United States, it has got to do it directly and not through the intermediation of these gentlemen. Every time it has come to a critical question these gentlemen have been yielded to, and their demands have been treated as the demands that should be followed as a matter of course.
>
> The government of the United States at present is a foster-child of the special interests. It is not allowed to have a will of its own. It is told at every move: 'Don't do that; you will interfere with our prosperity'. And when we ask, 'Where is our prosperity lodged?' a certain group of gentlemen say, 'With us.'

There could hardly be a better, more precise or more authoritative description of a plutocratic oligarchy in action. Two years later, Wilson was President of the United States and intent on taking the country to war. 'The world must be made safe for democracy,' he announced to Congress on April 2nd 1917. Since he himself had noted that America was not run by 'the people' but by business interests, he might have said with more honesty: 'the world must be made safe for American business interests.'

---

[46]   Part-quoted in Charles Beard, *The Republic*, p. 220. According to Élie Halévy, Britain had also become a plutocracy by this time: see his *History of the English People*, Epilogue 1, pp. 38-40.

To sum up: the myth of 'representative democracy' served a useful purpose by providing a rationale for stable middle-class government at a time when the *demos* was un-educated: but whatever its merit in the past, the myth needs challenging now. Everywhere we see nations under 'repre-sentative' governments driven by the worst impulses of reckless consumerism, media and social engineering, de-stroying culture, individuality, community and the natural world in the name of economic growth and progress. Huge gulfs develop between rich and poor (see Chapter 4); and meanwhile we (the people) are told that this is what we want. Whether 'we' want it or not, we are going to get it, for we are not in charge. Our 'democracy' is a myth.

How to introduce some true democracy into the modern world is the subject of the last chapter of this book: the next chapter is devoted to examining how electoral representa-tion has performed in England, the country which intro-duced it as a form of government to the modern world.

Chapter Three

Representative Government as a Home-Grown Product

The fundamental idea of 'representative democracy' is that the people, via their representatives, are the sovereign power. On the face of it this is a plausible story: representatives, chosen by popular vote, can change the laws in whatever way they choose and they also direct the operations of government.

Simple stories often mask a very different reality. Chapters One and Two have argued that democracy is fundamentally incompatible with representation: if we choose others to rule us, we are not doing the ruling ourselves. But if government by elected representatives is not democracy, what is it? The obvious answer is 'elective oligarchy', meaning that we are ruled by a fairly small number of people whom we choose to do the job of ruling for us. This, however, suggests two more questions: First, how much power do representatives really have? And second, do representatives act in the interests of 'the people'?

Representative government follows a pattern all of its own—a pattern very familiar to most of us, because it is our everyday reality. Although elected representatives are supposed to be the ruling power we see them coming and going while the true powers in our lives—political parties, bureaucracies, business corporations, the media, institutions of law and justice, quangos, international treaty agreements, financial systems, regulators etcetera—get on with business. We experience regular shocks when it comes to our notice that representatives are more bound in with these powers than with us, whom they are supposed to represent.

It is hardly surprising, however, that these powers survive the temporary dominions and tinkerings of elected representatives. Government, to be any good at all, relies on continuity as well as change. If these more permanent powers are well-constituted (so that they act in the public interest) then we are all the better for them; if not, we are all the worse. Elected representatives affect and to some extent direct these powers, but the powers have their own momentum. To use a racing analogy, the public may get to choose who rides the horse, but the trainers, the owners and the horse itself—let alone the track and the weather—are beyond their control.

As for the question 'who do representatives represent, the powers-that-be or the people?' the answer must clearly be an ever-changing see-saw. At election time, policies put to voters have been pre-agreed behind the scenes by political parties: candidates are clearly representing their parties to the people. A process of seduction takes place. After elections, 'representing the people' has to compete with (enforced) loyalty to party, ambition and self-interest, the momentum of events, and satisfying the powers-that-be.

Representative government has accumulated a long history of its own and this history illustrates its nature better than any theorizing. Aspects of its style and its workings emerge more clearly by looking at it over a long period, rather than from a glance at just last week or last year.

The origins of representative government lie in the European parliaments of the Middle Ages. Monarchs wanted to know what was going on among the peoples they ruled over: they summoned representatives 'to speak and make things known'.[1] There were many reasons for monarchs wanting to know what was going on. Even the worst king

---

[1]   'Ad loquendum or ad ostendendum': see M.V. Clarke, *Medieval Representation and Consent*, pp. 286-9.

wanted to avoid rebellion. Monarchs wanted to assess how much money could be extracted for their own use — for wars, luxury and administration. Also, they needed the allegiance of 'the people' in order to restrain the nobles — their constant rivals — from getting too much power.[2] Wars between nobles and monarchs were the recurring curse of the Middle Ages.

The idea behind representation was simple: in modern-day language, representatives carried information. Ordinary people *presented* information to the representative, who then *re-presented* it (presented it once again) to the monarch.[3] Representatives also carried information from the monarch back to the people: demands, concessions, responses to petitions.

Stubbs, the great constitutional historian, remarked that in every European country representatives began to be included in national assemblies at roughly the same time. 'The first recorded appearance of town representatives in the Cortes of Aragon is placed in 1162; the first in Castile in 1169. The general courts of Frederick of Sicily were framed in 1232; in Germany the cities appear by deputies in the Diet in 1255, in France the States General are called together first in 1302.'[4]

Alone of these medieval parliaments, the parliament of England evolved into a mode of government where representatives were supreme. Other medieval parliaments wasted away. Stubbs continues: 'In France, the States General were so managed as to place the whole realm under royal absolutism; in Spain the long struggle ended in the sixteenth century in making the king despotic... The Sicilian

---

[2]   In the words of May McKisack: 'to strike a financial bargain, to obtain information on specific points, to test the feeling of the country generally, or to obtain the support of numbers for a policy.' *The Parliamentary Representation of the English Boroughs During the Middle Ages* (1932), p. x.

[3]   'The representatives of the vills make presentments to a jury of twelve free-holders which represents the hundred, and then such of these presentments as the twelve jurors are willing to "avow," or make their own, are presented by them to the sheriff.' Maitland, *History of English Law Before Edward I* (1968 reprint p. 643). Maitland is describing the origins of political representation in judicial process.

[4]   *The Constitutional History of England* Chapter XV.

policy of Frederick passed away with his House; in Germany the disruption of all central government was reflected in the Diet…real life was diverted into provincial channels and dynastic designs.'[5]

In England, however, the House of Commons overcame first the power of the monarchy, then the power of the nobility, then the influence of the church. The process was gradual and by degrees. It took place over a period of five hundred years, starting around the middle of the thirteenth century. Because of the international importance of representative government, this history has been much written about by foreign as well as by British historians.[6] They have marked out significant moments on the journey made by representatives from humble 'presenters of information' to 'holders of sovereign power'.[7]

An early step was in 1265, when representatives were called not just to 'speak and make things known' but also to stay and attend Council in session. The motive was not some far-sighted vision of all-inclusive government. The summons was sent out (in the captive King's name) by a rebel leader, Simon de Montfort, who wanted to secure the continued financial help of the middle classes against the King.[8]

A further stage was in 1295, when representatives gained an element of formal power. This was not power over the monarch or the barons: it was power over those whom they represented. Edward I wanted representatives to attend for the same reason as Simon de Montfort: access to money.[9]

---

[5] For a more recent account see Marongiou, *Medieval Parliaments* (1968).

[6] Stubbs, Dicey, Maitland, and M.V. Clarke are some notable English writers; Guizot, Gienst, Gierke, Vinogradoff and White some of the notable foreign ones. The account that follows relies on these authorities and on Tasswell-Langmead's *Constitutional History* (10th edition).

[7] 'Sovereign power', meaning final authority, can in practice signify anything from merely nominal to absolute (totalitarian) power.

[8] 'To Simon, Earl of Leicester, belongs the lasting glory of having been the first to admit within the pale of our political constitution the really popular and progressive burgher class.' Tasswell-Langmead's *Constitutional History:* 10th edition, p. 150. See also Maddicott, *Simon de Montfort* (1996).

[9] See, for instance, G.W.S. Barrow, *Feudal Britain*, p. 300: 'If we ask why the parliaments of Edward I came, with ever greater frequency, to be at-

Representatives were wealthy men elected by other wealthy men. Edward I demanded that representatives come to parliament with full power (*plena potestas*) to bind the people they represented to what was agreed in 'common council' so that what was agreed there was 'not left undone'.[10] In other words, the king demanded that the people of England regard their representatives as agents acting on their behalf: what was agreed by their representatives would be legally and morally binding on the people.[11]

Representatives in medieval parliaments were far from the inner circle of power. The national executive was an 'inner council' chosen by the king. A larger 'great council', made up of nobles and churchmen, was called by the monarch from time to time to advise and give consent. When middle-class representatives attended, they stood in a corner while nobles and church dignitaries sat spaced around the room.[12] This great council became 'parliament' by the inclusion of representatives of the commons.[13]

After another two and a half centuries, representatives established themselves as indispensable to government business and thereby as a power to be reckoned with. This occurred under the Tudors, and in particular under Henry VIII—famous for his many wives, some of whom he had

---

tended by representatives of the shires and boroughs, the answer seems to be that especially for fiscal purposes, and to a less extent for political and legislative purposes, the king required the assent of men who had full power to bind the communities they represented, whether to a levy of taxation, or in support of the king's decision to go to war, or (less certainly in Edward I's time), in approval of a fresh statute.'

10   Gaines Post, 'Plena Potestas and Consent in Medieval Assemblies' in *Traditio* Vol. 1, (1943), pp. 355-408. The classic account of how the wording was reached is in J.G. Edwards, *Plena Potestas*, reprinted in *Historical Studies of the English Parliament* (1970). See also Maude Clarke, *Medieval Representation and Consent* (1936). 'Common council' consisted of king, nobles, magnates and representatives.

11   Maitland, *History of English Law Before Edward I* (1968 reprint, p. 228.)

12   Fascinating contemporary illustrations are reproduced in Pollard, *The Evolution of Parliament* (1920).

13   Maitland discusses the detail of this in *The Constitutional History of England* (1932) pp. 69ff.

killed, and for stealing the immense wealth of the monasteries. In these and many other offences Henry needed a partner.[14] 'With nearly half the peers, and at least four-fifths of the clergy, against him, Henry had need of the House of Commons, and he cultivated it with sedulous care.'[15] The House of Commons proved generally willing to 'cover his more outrageous proceedings with a convenient and plausible appearance of popular approbation':[16] and not only of approbation, but also of legality. Though a despot, Henry 'was yet animated by a scrupulous regard for the letter of the law.'[17] When he wanted to commit an offence he would request the House of Commons to change the law so that his intended crime would be legal. When for instance he wanted someone killed, the House of Commons would oblige him with an Act of Attainder, judicially murdering the victim without need of evidence or jury. The House of Commons was enjoying more power than it had ever enjoyed before.[18]

In this way, representatives of the middle classes became powerful by serving a greater power, jigging and re-writing the laws to suit their master. There were pay-offs: land and wealth stolen from the dead and from the monasteries was sold cheaply by the crown to members of the House of Commons. Candidates began to pay rather than be paid for election, beginning 350 years during which representatives openly attended the House of Commons for their own profit.[19]

After the Tudors, Stuart kings tried to impose upon England the model of government which was then being fashioned in continental Europe: absolute monarchy underwritten by 'the divine right of kings.'[20] Medieval theories of

---

[14]   Pollard (1920) pp. 321-2; also Maitland, *The Constitutional History of England* (1932) pp. 181*ff.*

[15]   Pollard (1920), p. 322.

[16]   Tasswell-Langmead, 10th Edition p 247.

[17]   Tasswell-Langmead, 10th Edition p. 246*ff*, 260*ff*; Pollard (1920) 321*ff*.

[18]   Emphasised in Freeman, The Growth of The English Constitution (1876).

[19]   Pollard (1920), p. 332.

[20]   Jean Bodin (1530-96) was its theorist (*The Six Bookes of a Commonweale*, trans. Richard Knolles (1962); i. 8, p. 98.). Cardinal Richelieu was an early

monarchy had given subjects the right of deposing an unjust monarch.[21] But in the new model of monarchy the king was appointed by God and parliaments were obsolete. The House of Commons, however, had gained in confidence and power. It had gained rights over authorizing and collecting taxation, and it had no intention of being relegated to obscurity.[22] The Stuart kings had neither the charismatic power of personality nor the popularity of the Tudors and the stage was set for a showdown between monarch and House of Commons.

Charles I, the second of the Stuart kings, tried ruling without parliament, but he ran out of money. 'Why did he not establish a paid army and bureaucracy like his French counterpart?' asks S.E Finer. 'The answer is obvious: he had no resources that would have remotely made this possible, because they lay in the hands of the House of Commons, that is, the gentry.'[23] The gentry not only dominated the House of Commons; they were the everyday administration of the country: justices of the peace, lawyers, sheriffs, bailiffs, squires of the manor.

It is interesting that during the conflicts which followed, none of the voices we might call 'democratic' – i.e. asserting that political power should be given to the common people – had anything to do with the House of Commons.[24] The House of Commons was fighting against tyranny to be sure,

---

proponent, justifying his immense power as an agent of the divinely-appointed King Louis XIII.

[21] See, for instance, Fritz Kern: *Kingship and Law in the Middle Ages* (1968).

[22] 'As well as voting supplies of money to 'His Majesty' it also appropriated those supplies.' Maitland, 'The Crown as Corporation' in *State, Trust and Corporation* (2003), p. 42. 'The very fact that the Tudor Kings had found Parliaments subservient, and had therefore used them, had given Parliaments a great place in the State', J.R. Tanner, *English Constitutional Conflicts of the Seventeenth Century*, (1928), pp. 5-6.

[23] The History of Government, (1997), p.138.

[24] See for example texts in *A Radical Reader* (2006) ed. Christopher Hampton: e.g. 'when you the commonalty calleth forth a Parliament they are confident such must be chosen that are the noblest and richest… your slavery is their liberty, your poverty is their prosperity…' p. 178.

but not on behalf of the people: it was fighting for government by gentry as opposed to government by monarch. The democrat 'Honest John' Lilburne (whipped and imprisoned under King Charles I, imprisoned and banished by Parliament, imprisoned again then exiled by Oliver Cromwell) found tyranny by gentry worse than tyranny by monarch: 'I had rather live seven years under old King Charles' government than live one year under the present government that now rule', he told his parliamentary jailer.[25]

The victory of Parliament in the English Civil War and the subsequent execution of King Charles I was a defining moment in the ever-increasing power of the House of Commons. An assembly which can judicially kill a monarch is not to be trifled with. The House of Commons abolished not only royalty but also the House of Lords. In theory it was now ruling alone, but a fundamental problem arose immediately: the commons made the laws, but with the king gone, who would make up the executive? To answer this, the victorious army general — Cromwell — assembled an executive council just like the king used to do, choosing whom he wished for, from representatives, the army, the aristocracy and an assortment of significant individuals.

Cromwell summoned three new parliaments during his ten years of power and dismissed four, including the one he had fought for. Royalists and Catholics were excluded both from sitting in, and voting for, his new parliaments.[26] Not only Cromwell but also his contemporaries and later historians found these parliaments dithering, corrupt, fanatical, self-serving, intent on keeping power but incapable of exercising it responsibly, arrogant, unrealistic, keen to go to war with friends and fearful of true enemies. Each in turn was dismissed by Cromwell, and not many people missed them.

---

[25]   Guizot (1854), p. 64.
[26]   "Roman Catholics, royalists, and any who had 'advised, assisted or abetted the rebellion in Ireland' or 'any war against the Parliament' since 1 January 1642 were debarred from being either electors or elected." Little and Smith, *Parliaments and Politics during the Cromwellian Protectorate* (2007), p. 51.

Cromwell exercised despotic power and England was subjected to twelve years of military dictatorship known as 'the Commonwealth'. Ordinary people were morally supervised by military tribunals and punished for transgressing puritan standards of behaviour. Most forms of entertainment were banned (including Christmas) and the return of a monarch in 1660 – Charles II, son of the decapitated Charles I – was greeted with joy.[27]

The mockery of parliamentary government during 'the Commonwealth' pointed up a great and significant problem: a representative legislature was now established in custom and in law, but how was it possible to form a representative executive? The opportunity for an English solution to this problem arose eighty years later under a new dynasty and a German-born monarch (George I) keen on spending time in his native Hanover. Parliament, left rather more to its own devices, found it could choose its own executive appointed by (and largely from) the dominant party faction.[28] Political parties became more organised now that it was in their power to compose the executive. Loose and shifting alliances began to harden into the kinds of political machinery we are familiar with today.[29]

Parliament in the eighteenth century consisted of an aristocratic House of Lords and a middle-class House of Commons. The House of Commons allowed itself to be heavily corrupted by wealthy Lords who bought not just votes but seats – the 'rotten boroughs'. The aristocracy and the middle classes had a common interest in helping each other grow

---

[27]   The House of Lords, banned in 1649 as 'useless and dangerous', was also restored.

[28]   This dates from around the 1720's: in 1705, parliament repealed a clause in the Act of Settlement which prohibited MPs from serving as government ministers (Hennessy (2001), p. 40). Fifty years later (1776), the Americans would come up with a different solution to the problem: a separately elected presidential executive.

[29]   See Lewis Namier, *Monarchy and the Party System* (1952).

rich and most of their opportunities involved dispossessing the poor (who still had rights in land).[30]

Traditionally, the monarch had protected the poor, but the monarch was now largely irrelevant. The poor were left to the mercy of parliament, which in over three thousand privately-sponsored Acts of Enclosure (between 1700 and 1850) systematically dispossessed them of their rights. Over twenty-four percent of the land of Britain was taken out of the old system of common rights and enclosed by landlords.[31] Countryside and cities filled with the vagrant and the dispossessed.

Nowadays, when most people dwell in cities, it is sometimes forgotten how wealth-creating activities depend upon control and possession of land.[32] Not just food, but housing, office-space, industry, transport systems, sales outlets, mineral extraction, storage facilities, military activity, communications, recreation, tourism, energy, and almost every source of money and power still depend on access, ownership and control of land. Once the poor were deprived of rights in land they were helpless dependents upon employment or charity from those who had dispossessed them.[33]

The great enemy of enterprising capital is a self-sustaining life.[34] A family living a self-contained existence on a piece of land is profitable to no one.[35] Once the family is

---

[30] 'Aristocrat' is of course another misnomer. It derives from the Greek for 'rule by the best' — not a dominant theme in history.

[31] John Chapman, 'The Extent and Nature of Parliamentary Enclosure', *Agricultural History Review*, XXXV, 1 (1987), p. 28.

[32] For 21st century appropriations of land rights in cities, see *Ground Control* (2009) by Anna Minton.

[33] The rights of the poor in land were not usually rights of direct ownership, but rights to occupy. These rights were left over from feudal times, when all land was in theory held from the king. Freehold rights developed among the richer tenants, but the poor depended upon the protection of the monarch to resist encroachment from freeholders.

[34] Not for nothing is Faust's final crime (in Goethe's version) to murder a couple living in peaceful isolation. Faust, the quintessential modern man, justifies his final crimes with visions of 'progress'.

[35] This principle appears to extend to self-contained economies as well as self-contained individuals: America sent gunboats in 1853/4 to force Japan to open up to Western interests.

displaced, the land can be put to profit. Dispossessed adults can be 'gainfully employed' (whose gain?) and the whole family can be trained up—via advertising and the rest—as consumers. Lastly, in the peculiar perversity of modern economics, the illnesses, depressions, crimes and other discontents of the dependent are of immense profit to the pharmaceutical, insurance, care, security, manufacturing, entertainment and prison industries.

Classic books on the dispossession of the poor by parliament were written by the Hammonds, husband-and-wife writers, between 1911 and 1934.[36] Since they were written, huge amounts of work and research have extended the picture, making it more complex and occasionally contradicting the Hammonds.[37] Later writers have attempted to discredit their conclusions: their accounts have been labelled hysterical and misleading, and statistics have been misleadingly used to pretend that enclosures barely happened.[38]

In simple historical fact, driving the poor off the land was, off-and-on, a source of profit to landowners long before elected representatives gained sovereign power. When (as happened in the sixteenth century) landowners found sheep more profitable than humans, many landlords tried to force humans off and bring sheep in.[39] The monarch's interest, on

---

[36]   The Village Labourer 1760-1832: a Study of the Government of England before the Reform Bill (1911), The Town Labourer 1760-1832: The New Civilisation (1917) and The Skilled Labourer 1760-1832 (1919).

[37]   In particular, the monumental *Agrarian History of England and Wales* (2011) ed. Joan Thirsk.

[38]   On the misleading use of statistics see Joan Thirsk, *The Rural Economy of England* (1984), p. 13.

[39]   For instance Sir Thomas More, 1516: 'your sheep that were wont to be so meek and tame, and so small eaters, now, as I heard say, be become so great devourers and so wild, that they eat up, and swallow down the very men themselves. They consume, destroy, and devour whole fields, houses, and cities. For look in what parts of the realm doth grow the finest, and therefore dearest wool, there noble men, and gentlemen, yea and certain Abbots, holy men no doubt, not contenting themselves with the yearly revenues and profits, that were wont to grow to their forefathers and predecessors of their lands, nor being content that they live in rest and pleasure nothing profiting, yea much noying the weal public, leave no ground for tillage: they inclose all into pastures, they throw

the other hand, was to protect the poor: not just to avoid wandering crowds threatening peace and needing provision, but also because they were his natural allies against the nobility. When rule was in the hands of an assembly of wealthy individuals, however, there was no such restraining power. Privately-sponsored Acts of Parliament drove most of the remaining peasant cottagers and smallholders off the land, taking away their rights and allocating them to large landowners.[40]

During the eighteenth century, 'improvement' and 'progress' were held to justify these dispossessions. 'Improvement' and 'progress' meant more wealth for a few and the increased power of 'capital' to command life and labour. As for the poor, the effect on their lives was summed up by Joan Thirsk:

> Common fields and pastures kept alive a vigorous co-operative spirit in the community; enclosures starved it. In champion country [*i.e. open fields with rights of cultivation held in common*] people had to work together amicably, to agree upon crop rotations, stints of common pasture, the upkeep and improvement of their grazings and meadows, the clearing of ditches, the fencing of fields. They toiled side by side in the fields, and they walked together from field to village from farm to heath, morning, afternoon, and evening. They all depended on common resources for their fuel, for bedding, and fodder for their stock, and by pooling so many of the necessities of livelihood they were disciplined from early youth to submit to the rules and the customs of their community. After enclosure, when every man

---

down houses, they pluck down towns, and leave nothing standing, but only the church to be made a sheephouse.'

[40]   In her essay 'The Inclosure of Common Fields in the Seventeenth Century' E.M. Leonard examines the beginnings of this wave of enclosure which led to the destruction of rural society, as 'the possession of land became more exclusively the privilege of the rich'. She quotes Roger North's contemporary account, which refers to 'vast depopulations not ordinarily thought of or imagined possible'. Carus-Wilson ed., *Essays in Economic History Vol. II*, 1966. See also the Hammonds' *Village Labourer* (1911), Maurice Beresford's *The Lost Villages of England* (1998) and books by Joan Thirsk for the 18th and 19th centuries.

could fence his own piece of territory and warn his neighbours off, the discipline of sharing things fairly with one's neighbours was relaxed, and every household became an island to itself. This was the great revolution in men's lives, greater than all the economic changes following enclosure. Yet few people living in this world bequeathed to us by the enclosing and improving farmer are capable of gauging the full significance of a way of life that is now lost.

The appropriation, by one means or another, of lands owned or occupied by the poor continues. What was accomplished in England by legislation is being accomplished today all over the world by bank-created capital and debt-finance (see Chapter Four).

The treatment of the poor under electoral representation is the largest body of evidence against its claim to be democratic. As Aristotle pointed out more than two thousand years ago, if democracy means anything it means that the poor enjoy political sovereignty: for better or worse, the authority of the state is theirs.[41] Part of his logic is that the rich and the middle classes always have a certain amount of power anyway, as owners and administrators, but without true democracy the poor have no influence at all beyond the threat of riot, strike and rebellion.

The relentless assault by the middle classes on the poor resurfaces again and again whenever some form of community and well-being is detected among them, which seems to indicate that something greater than economic interest is at work: perhaps bad conscience, perhaps what Oakeshott called the 'mindless passion to destroy what it can never appropriate' (in this case a sense of community), perhaps merely the anxiety that the poor majority will wake up one day and decide not to submit any more to the 'relentless war' against them.[42] Enclosure — dispossession — played its

---

[41] *Politics* IV, 4. 'The form of government is a democracy when the free, who are also poor and the majority, govern.' Tr. Jowett, available online. Another translation: 'a democracy is a state where the freemen and the poor, being the majority, are invested with the power of the state.'

[42] Preserved Smith's phrase (*The Age of the Reformation* (1920) p. 556).

part in the 'atomisation' of society which so bothered Victorians, and which we live with today.

In England, where the practice of dispossession was pioneered, the poor are now confined in sink 'housing estates' rarely visited by outsiders unless they are members of the helping professions. Estates in towns are notorious places of deprivation. In the countryside, they are fenced off, their inhabitants forbidden to walk on the land let alone set up smallholdings.[43] Under medieval law, if cottagers or squatters could put up a dwelling on unused land within twenty-four hours, the cottage and a number of surrounding acres would be theirs to occupy by right.

For centuries, the same arguments have been used to justify dispossession of the poor: progress, enhanced productivity and concern (or contempt) for their supposed incapacity. Things said openly in the eighteenth century are said today behind closed doors. The poor are said to be bettered by dispossession: once their land is stolen, all the opportunities of civilization are supposedly open to them.[44] In the words of the Hammonds, 'the poor never lost a right without being congratulated by the rich for gaining something better.'[45]

History points up the fact that people can only be trusted, as a statistical generalization with few exceptions, to act in what they perceive to be their own best interests. Until the late nineteenth century, poor people were generally denied the vote in representative assemblies. This changed early in the twentieth century. In England, poor men were given the vote in 1918 and poor women in 1928. In the United States, where the franchise is determined by individual states, the situation is compromised by practical mechanisms used to prevent sections of the population from voting (such as making polling booths difficult to access). But the drift has been

---

[43] Attempts to change this via legislation result only in greater restriction: the so-called 'right to roam', for instance, only applies to 'mountain, moor, heath, down and registered common land'. As a result, smallholdings in England are generally second homes for middle-class owners.

[44] J.D. Chambers quoted by Joan Thirsk: *The Rural Economy of England* (1984), p. 13.

[45] *The Village Labourer* (1911), p. 109.

everywhere the same, towards universal adult franchise. When suffrage includes the poor, there is at least a semblance of justification to the idea of representatives acting on behalf of 'all of the people'. So to what extent did representatives adopt the interests of the poor?

Being a representative is a middle-class job. A few will have roots among the poor and even fewer may retain some loyalty to them.[46] But the world in which representatives move, their ambitions and their party masters all embody powerful interests that, while they may claim to consider the poor, are not of the poor. Why should anyone believe that a particular group of people, contrary to all evidence of history, acts against its own interests? So what happened after universal franchise, when middle-class political candidates had to appeal to the poor majority?[47]

In 1879, during the progress towards to universal adult franchise, F.W. Maitland worried that as the franchise expanded the elite would be able to get away with a great deal more than they did already. If voters did not take a close interest in everyday law, he said, they would never know how it disadvantaged them, and if they did not exert pressure for change, then change would not happen:

> Little will now be done by Parliament to which it is not urged from without, and in these days, when there are always many excellent and exciting electioneering cries, many questions about which it is easy to make a stir, no Minister could afford to

---

46 The situation has not substantially changed since Michels' *Political Parties* (1911).

47 The public enemies of 'representative democracy' in the twentieth century were the various totalitarianisms — fascism, Nazism, communism. These were out-and-out fusions of tyranny and oligarchy, unabashedly offering to put control of society in the hands of party elites. Occasional pretensions to being 'democratic' were in retrospect entirely bogus. Totalitarian governments are an extreme form of representative government: their elites claim to represent the interests of 'the people' but their claims are belied by the various forms of violence used to maintain power and their intolerance of rival parties, publicity, emigration, and all forms of opposition. They are not in any sense of the word 'democratic' and they are not the subject of this book, which is the undemocratic nature of freely-contested representative government.

devote Session after Session to measures for which there was no popular demand.[48]

As if in direct fulfilment of F.W. Maitland's concern, after poor people got the vote the principal mechanism operating directly against their interests expanded massively in scope and power. The creation of money by banks in favour of capitalists, which by 1920 was accepted and understood fact, expanded greatly as an active process in the economy.[49] Whereas early in the twentieth century about 30% of the money supply in Western nations was created by banks, the figure now is consistently over 95%.

Whether you take the popular adage 'money is power in its most liquid form' or listen to the historians — 'power follows property' — an obvious job for any elite that wants to stay in power is to corner the money supply. Under representative government, this has proved remarkably easy. Tricks 'hardly worthy of even a third-rate magician'[50] have been used to buy up the world, reducing the independent poor to penury and the majority of citizens to dependence on governments, corporations and the ultra-rich. It was made all the easier by the tricks-of-the-trade being ready to hand: people had been using them for hundreds, even thousands of years. All that was needed was to stop mentioning them, give them free rein, and hope no one would notice.

'Credit creation' by banks has become the major source of new money, which now exists almost entirely as debt (from people to banks and from banks to customers, with an interest differential between the two). The name 'credit creation' is something of a disguise: the device feeds money to the rich at the expense of the poor. Representatives have keep silent about this mechanism and allowed it to expand until almost all of our money is created this way. Like so many others,

---

48 'The Law of Real Property' in *Collected Papers 1*, Liberty Fund edition, p. 79.

49 At roughly the same time several pieces of work established beyond controversy that what had been denied for some time was in fact the case: C.A. Phillips (1920), F.W. Crick (1927), Keynes (1930).

50 W.J. Thorne, *Banking* (1948), p. 133.

they protect themselves with ignorance, in fear lest the whole shopping cart of Western finance be upended.[51]

The mechanism by which almost all of our money is created is examined in the next chapter.

---

[51] The very respectable Lloyd Mints, historian of banking, remarked in an interview on his 100th birthday (available currently on youtube): 'The centre of ignorance is Congress'. (He was recommending an end not to credit, but to credit creation.)

Chapter Four

Case Study: How Debt Came to Rule the World

Human nature is ready and willing to heap up riches whenever it easily can, so eventually the powerful may get hold of everyone else's money and reduce them to slavery. This is tyranny indeed: true and absolute tyranny, as described by the philosophers and in ancient history. – *Nicole Oresme, 14th C, on abusing the money supply.*

The purpose of studying economics is not to acquire a set of readymade answers to economic questions, but to avoid being deceived by economists. – *Joan Robinson, economist.*

Of all betrayals of 'the people' made by elected representatives, allowing banks to create the money supply has been the greatest.[1] Case studies could be made of other areas in which representatives serve elites rather than ordinary people (e.g. culture, education, the arms trade, the environment, war, intellectual property, oil and energy, corporate rights); I

---

[1] It would be more correct to call banks 'depository institutions'. Legal privileges first allowed to banks have now been extended to other types of institution. For instance in the U.S. the Depository Institutions Deregulation and Monetary Control Act (1980) extended banking privileges to federal credit unions. 'All depository institutions are subject to the reserve requirements set by the Federal Reserve. Thus all such institutions, not just commercial banks, have the potential for creating money.' – *Modern Money Mechanics,* Federal Reserve Bank of Chicago (online). It seems simpler, however, to adopt the common designation and refer to institutions possessing 'banker's privilege' as 'banks'.

have chosen bank-created money because control of the money supply is fundamental to all power.

The subject occupies a substantial chapter in itself because as well as telling the story of how the world has become so unequal, it exposes how powerful interests operate beyond public knowledge and democratic scrutiny. It also shows how privilege has become so much part of what 'just goes on', that the powerful themselves may live in denial, or even ignorance, of how they are privileged.

Legal accommodation of bank-created money began six years after representatives assumed supreme power in England (the dates are 1688 and 1694). Over the next three hundred years, bank-created money came to dominate the money supply of the world, as other countries followed in England's footsteps. It is impossible to understand how such a strange system came to be without a bit of history; but first it is intriguing to see how the system works today.

Beneath all the complex talk, the truth about bank-created money is not so complex. In the words of banker W.J. Thorne 'the banker's tricks of the trade are, when they are explained, hardly worthy of even a third-rate magician.'[2]

The magic trick of banking is to lend the same money again and again. Normally, if you lend something, it is gone and you no longer have it. But bankers are able to produce money they have already lent like a rabbit out of a hat, and lend it again. The trick depends on several special privileges given to banks in law.

The first and fundamental privilege of banks is to own deposits of money put with them for safe-keeping. This privilege was re-stated (rather impatiently and in no uncertain terms) by a judge, Lord Cottenham, in 1848:

> Money, when paid into a bank, ceases altogether to be the money of the customer; it is then the money of the banker, who is bound to return an equivalent by paying a similar sum to that

---

2   W.J. Thorne (B.Com, Associate of the Institute of Bankers) in *Banking* (OUP) 1948. Mervyn King, ex-Chairman of the Bank of England, prefers the word 'alchemy': see his 'Speech to the Buttonwood Gathering, New York, 25 October 2010' available on the Bank of England website.

deposited with him when he is asked for it. ... [It] is to all intents and purposes the money of the banker, to do with it as he pleases. He is guilty of no breach of trust in employing it; he is not answerable to the customer if he puts it into jeopardy, if he engages in a hazardous speculation; he is not bound to keep it or deal with it as the property of the customer, but he is, of course, answerable for the amount, because he has contracted, having received that money, to repay to the customer, when demanded, a sum equivalent to that paid into his hands.[3]

In other words, as soon as you deposit your money in a bank it becomes the property of the bank. What you have in return is a claim on an equivalent amount of the bank's cash.

It is a strange, perhaps unique quality of money that *claims* on money can themselves be used as money. The economist Joseph Schumpeter pointed out the oddity of this.[4] If you need a horse to get to market, a claim on a horse is not enough: you need the actual horse. But if, when you get to market, your pockets are stuffed full of claims on money, you can use them to pay with by simply handing your claim to someone else. In other words, claims on money are themselves money. Almost all our payments today are made this way. Cheques, credit card payments, debit card payments merely transfer some of our claim on a bank's money to someone else.[5]

The fact that claims on money are themselves money allows the magic trick of banking to really take off. A bank creates money by creating claims. Here's how it works.

---

3   Foley v Hill, (1848). This was not the first statement of the fundamental banker's privilege. It has become famous because it is so direct and unequivocal.

4   *A History of Economic Analysis,* p. 321. The scattered chapters on money, credit, banking etc. in this mighty book provided some of the material for these paragraphs.

5   Knut Wicksell pointed out over a hundred years ago that modern economies are hybrids of two systems, cash and 'credit' (*Interest and Prices,* 1898: English translation 1936, page 70). Keynes, under a subheading 'Current Money is predominantly Bank-Money' (*Treatise on Money,* Chapter 2) estimated that 90% of money in use by the public at that date (1930) was bank-created claims. Now (2012) the percentage is consistently over 97%.

A bank extends a loan: the borrower now has a claim against the bank. When the borrower spends some of the loan, some of his claim passes to another person. The new person might bank at the same bank, in which case cash leaves and returns to the bank in a 'scintilla of time'; or the new person might bank at a different bank, in which case the bank loses some of its cash to the other bank. However, loans are created (and spent) every day at all banks, and at the end of each day's trading the banks tally up what they owe to each other (the process is known as 'clearing'). The various claims between them (usually) roughly even out.[6] Inequalities are met by short-term borrowing through the clearing banks.[7]

So a loan of cash is like a magic boomerang: cash leaves the banking system and returns again, creating on its journey a debt (from the borrower to the bank) and new claims on the bank's cash, owned by people the borrower has paid. The result is not all roses for the bank. If we take stock of where the bank is after making a loan, we can see that it has become vulnerable. There are new claims on its cash, but the cash is not there to back them up. When banks create bad debts, claims pile up on cash that isn't there: they are preparing for their own funeral (or for the modern luxury of a state bail-out).

So money is created by banks in the form of two debts: from banks to customers, and from borrowers to banks.

---

6   Wicksell describes the process thus: 'The sum borrowed today in order to buy commodities is placed by the seller of the goods on his account at the same bank or some other bank, and can be lent the very next day to some other person with the same effect.' 'The Influence of the Rate of Interest on Prices', 1907.

7   'Clearing' means the banking system as a whole behaves as if it were one single bank, with a monopoly. Interestingly, the process depends upon all banks behaving in roughly the same way; otherwise, a 'multiple-lending' bank would quickly lose its money to other banks, as borrowers make payments. For a short summary of the process from a banker's point of view see 'The Theory Of Multiple Expansion Of Deposits: What It Is And Whence It Came' by Thomas M. Humphrey, *Economic Review* March/April 1987. Available online at the Federal Bank of Richmond website.

When a loan is 'retired' — that is, repaid — these debts, which are mirror-images of each other, get smaller by equal amounts. Money is literally destroyed, in the same way it was created but in reverse: the borrower accumulates claims then turns them over to the ownership of the bank, which uses them to claim cash from other banks. Cash shuffles between banks after which the claims are redundant: they no longer exist.

It is no coincidence that the word 'bubble' crops up so frequently in stories of bank-created money: bank-money is itself a bubble. It is made and it is destroyed, leaving nothing behind it but a transfer of assets to capitalists and banks.[8]

The loans have paid the banks interest.[9] Because they create many loans on the same cash, banks earn many times the interest they could hope for on the same cash if they were straightforward moneylenders. For this reason, they can lend at lower rates of interest than straightforward moneylenders (who have occupied a niche corner of the market for several centuries now — lending at high rates to the poor). Low interest rates, and a plentiful supply of created money, give bank-borrowers an advantage in the marketplace; and this advantage depends on the privilege of banks to create money for lending.

The result is that our money supply consists of two entirely separate systems: one of cash, almost all of it owned by governments and banks; [10] and the other of claims-on-cash, owned by the rest of us. These two systems are given a variety of different names by different agencies and different

---

8   The words 'capital' and 'capitalist' suffer from long association with Marxist critique. Before Marx, there was sensible and constructive criticism of capitalism; now, criticism tends to conjure up visions of totalitarianism.

9   Banks also *pay* interest to some depositors; the difference between the interest they pay and the interest they receive is the primary income of banks.

10   Actual coins and notes make up a very small percentage of the money supply – usually around 3%. They are 'cash' and governments and banks like to discourage their use. If all citizens asked for the money due to them in cash tomorrow, governments and banks would collapse — or the system would have to undergo instant reform!

economists. 'Cash' is known as 'the monetary base' (acronym MB), 'state money' and 'high-powered money'. Claims are given an even wider variety of names: 'near-money', 'money substitute', 'representative money', 'fiduciary money', 'credit money', 'bank-money'. Following Keynes and Schumpeter (among others) I use 'cash' and 'claims', not only because are they familiar ideas, but because they describe accurately what is going on.[11]

Cash circulates between banks, central banks and treasury accounts, only leaking out a little to the general public in the form of government-issued notes and coins.[12] One of its names, 'high-powered money', is revealing. By creating new cash, and buying government debt from banks, governments feed cash into the system in the hope that it will stimulate banks to loan more claims (this is called quantitative easing). This does not always work, however. Banks like to lend when times are good and loans are productive. When times are bad, they call loans in: the process of money-creation goes into reverse and money is destroyed.[13] This is known by economists as the 'perverse elasticity' of bank-created money.[14]

The monetary system, which could be relatively simple if it consisted of cash, is made complicated by the huge variety of claims that can legally be used as money.[15] Claims are

---

[11]   Even though it was written in the days of the gold standard when claims could be redeemed in actual silver-and-gold, C.A. Phillips, *Bank Credit* (1920) is by far the best explanation I have come across of what actually goes on in a banking system. Since modern banking is a virtual reproduction of the system he describes the book is still vital reading. It is downloadable at mises.org.

[12]   Notes and coins are sold to banks by the government and provided to customers of banks on demand. Once in circulation, they are however independent of the banking system.

[13]   See above (p. 50) for how it is destroyed.

[14]   E.g. Simons, (1948) p. 65; Lester (1939) p. 291.

[15]   Simons looked forward to 'an economy where all private property consisted in pure assets, pure money and nothing else. This, along with fiscal stabilization of the value of money, is the financial good society.' *Economics for a Free Society* p. 239. If sanity made a sudden appearance in human affairs, such a state would not be hard to achieve.

sub-categorised by type: claims that can be realised quickly, claims with a time delay, claims with special conditions attached (such as specific events occurring), claims on claims (derivatives) and so forth. The various official ways of measuring the money supply—M1-6, MZM, and so on—differ according to what kinds of claims are included in the measuring.[16] The tricks of financial acquisition by which speculators get rich are built on elaborately improvised claims, backed by state recognition of claims as legal tender, a recognition first made in the Promissory Notes Act of 1704.

Our bizarre system is far from being the only way that money can be created (others will be looked at later in this chapter) and it is now manifestly a malignant one. How did such a bizarre system come to be?

The story of bank-created money is a story of governments accommodating dubious practices for their own advantage, and it reveals who are the winners and who are the losers of the system.

Banking is one of the oldest professions known to man (the oldest is said to be prostitution) and abuses of banking trust have been detected as far back as ancient Mesopotamia.[17] Systems of law from early times wrestled with two especially risky banking habits: the tendency of bankers to speculate with money they hold in safe-keeping, and the practice of issuing claims on more money than they have in

---

[16] M0 (or MB) measures cash only; when governments start creating more cash, they become reticent about publishing figures for these measurements, as have the U.S. and U.K. governments recently.

[17] Michael Jones, *Creative Accounting, Fraud and International Accounting Scandals*, p. 117.

store.[18] Modern banking is the legal accommodation, development and management of these ancient habits.[19]

The modern story begins in the 17th century, at a time when money consisted of gold and silver coin (and cheaper metal alloy for small denominations). Being made of something valuable in itself, money consisted of wealth that already existed. Gold and silver bullion would be brought by its owners to the Mint and converted into coin, the monarch's stamp certifying it as currency.[20] Monarchs made a profit ('seigniorage') and owners of the bullion made a profit too: they would only bring in bullion when it would be worth more as coin. The profits were usually one-off of a few percent.[21] The system could be abused: for instance, monarchs could call in the currency, re-make it with cheaper metal and pocket the difference.[22] But in general, the process of money creation was roughly neutral, in that it did not make the rich much richer or the poor much poorer.

The men blamed (or praised) for kicking-off modern banking are the English 'goldsmith bankers' who began lending claims on gold they didn't have.[23] These men were

---

[18]   The two habits result in the same outcome: claims on more cash than bankers have in store. Abbott Payson Usher examines banking practice in relation to various systems of law in *The Early History of Deposit Banking in Mediterranean Europe* (Harvard UP, 1943); see also Raymond de Roover, 'New Interpretations of the History of Banking' in *Business, Banks and Economic Thought* (1974).

[19]   Usher (op. cit.) stresses that multiple lending was practiced long before the goldsmith bankers: for instance, in the early 15th century Barcelona's Bank of Deposit 'was capable of extending credit in the ratio of 3.3 times the reserves on hand' (p.181). The significant development of English banking was managed cooperation between banks and elected representatives in government.

[20]   See *The Pound Sterling* by Albert Feaveryear (OUP 1963).

[21]   Feaveryear's *The Pound Sterling* Chapters 1 and 5.

[22]   Certain monarchs became notorious for this: Henry VIII, for instance, added it to his already long list of historical sins.

[23]   Innumerable textbooks and articles on economics and banking tell the tale: for instance, Baumol and Blinder *Economics: Principles & Policy* (2009, p. 632); Greg Mankiw *Principles of Economics* (2008, p. 650), Robert Laurent in *Federal Reserve Bank of Chicago Economic Perspectives* (March 1994, p. 4).

thorough-going members of the English establishment: among them Sir Jeremiah Snow, Sir Robert Vyner (Lord Mayor of London, 1653-4), and Alderman Edward Backwell, MP.[24] Goldsmiths began their banking careers during the insecurity of the English Civil War, when some of them found there was more profit in storing gold for other people than in making things out of gold themselves. When they took deposits of other people's gold they would issue paper receipts, and these receipts — claims on gold — began to circulate as methods of payment. In other words, claims began to circulate as money.[25]

People also came to these ex-goldsmiths to borrow gold: but instead of taking away actual gold, they too preferred to take away paper claims. These claims were the same as the ones given to depositors.[26] There was an obvious temptation in this for the new bankers — to lend claims on gold they didn't actually possess.[27] So long as claimants didn't all turn

---

[24] From the Goldsmith's Company website (20/01/2012): 'Several leading goldsmiths who had for some time past been keeping 'running-cashes' in order to be able to lend money to their customers at short notice now all but abandoned the practice of making and selling plate in order to run full-time banking houses, and the promissory notes they issued formed the style of our first bank notes. Prominent members of the Goldsmiths' Company such as Sir Robert Vyner, Sir Jeremiah Snow, Alderman Edward Backwell, Valentine Duncomb and Robert Blanchard made vast fortunes in their new businesses.'

[25] '"The notes of goldsmiths (whether they be payable to order or to bearer) are always accounted among merchants as ready cash, and not as bills of exchange," Tassell and Lee v. Lewis (1696) 1 Ld. Raym. at p. 744.' Quoted in Holdsworth, *A History of English Law* (1926, p. 191 n.9).

[26] Good accounts of this are in Richards, *The Early History of Banking in England* and Horsefield, *British Monetary Experiments* 1650-1710.

[27] 'The last step in the evolution of the bank-note was the discovery by the goldsmith that, as his promises to pay on demand passed from hand to hand as the equivalent of coin supposed to be behind them, so he might, on the faith of his own credit, issue promises to pay on demand that had no foundation of the precious metals as their basis.' J.B. Martin, *The Grasshopper in Lombard Street*, p. 127. 'There is, also, documentary evidence which shows that the goldsmith's promissory note which was not actually backed by gold had made its appearance in the early years of the post-Restoration regime.' Richards, *The Early History of Banking in England*, p.230.

up at once to claim the actual gold, the scam would never be discovered. Meanwhile, the bankers charged real interest on pretend money. These men were already involved in many illegal practices (coin clipping, melting down overweight coins to sell as metal, lending at rates above legal limits) so it would have been strange if they had passed up on such an obvious opportunity.

There was a further incentive: having lent money that didn't exist, they found themselves being repaid in money that did exist. So long as the paper claims kept circulating as money, the gold they represented would stay unclaimed in the bankers' vaults. The borrower would pay back the loan in gold or in paper claims — either of which could be used as money. Those early bankers rapidly became extremely rich.[28] The practical consideration for these early English bankers was what it has remained for bankers ever since: how many claims be lent on the same money without inviting the disaster of a 'run on the bank' — that is, of everyone turning up at once to claim money, most of which isn't there?

There were obviously several types of fraud (or near-fraud) in the practice. It is lending a claim on something you don't have. It is taking money (interest payments and loan re-payments) under false pretences. It is diluting the value of currency held by others — a schoolboy's dream, taking a little from everyone so they won't notice. It is manufacturing money for your own benefit.

So far, the story is just another tale of dodgy bankers sailing close to the wind. Instead of outlawing their tricks, however, successive English governments first ignored them, then made use of them, and then passed laws to accommodate them. The system which emerged, of cooperation be-

---

[28]   For instance: 'Duncomb, not long since a mean goldsmith, having made a purchase of the late Duke of Buckingham's estate at neere £90,000 and reputed to have neere as much in cash' (Evelyn's Diary, 11 June 1696).The stages in the evolution of the goldsmith 'into a banker in the modern sense' are summarised in Richards, *The Early History of Banking in England*, Chapter IX (iv).

tween government and banks, is the system of modern
banking and finance — and of government borrowing.

The injustices arising from this cooperation were widely
recognised at the time and there were vehement protests – of
which, more later. They was also recognised in popular
speech: the 'financial genius' of the seventeenth century,
who introduced the bill of incorporation of the Bank of England to Parliament, was popularly known as 'Filcher' Montague (filching means 'surreptitiously misappropriating the
assets of others').[29]

In retrospect, the government's accommodation of the
new practice is not surprising, for a number of reasons. First
of all, the rulers of England — the Stuart Kings, the dictator
Oliver Cromwell, then (after 1688) parliament — were constantly in need of cash, and not averse to acting dishonestly
themselves in financial matters: they found the bankers useful and convenient sources of lending.[30] Second, the frauds
fitted no established criminal category (they differed from
counterfeiting and theft in that money was only created in
the act of lending). Third, people with ambition were generally happy because the bankers offered them easy money at
better rates of interest. Fourth, it was not obvious at first who
were victims of the fraud; later, when it became obvious, the
victims were not strong enough to resist.[31] Fifth, there was at
that time a great demand for credit and money for capitalist
ventures, and bankers were thought to be contributing to the

---

[29]   Charles Montague, Earl of Halifax. From the *Encyclopedia Britannica* of
1911: 'It may be affirmed that no other statesman has initiated schemes
which have left a more permanent mark on the financial history of England.' Thomas Jefferson also referred to bankers as 'filchers' (letter to
John Adams, 24 Jan 1814).

[30]   'By the time James II fled England in 1688, the later Stuarts had compiled
a catalogue of arbitrary actions towards their creditors as lengthy and
disreputable as that of the earlier Stuarts.' Nichols, 'English Government
Borrowing 1660-1688' in *Journal of British Studies*, 10, 2 1971 p. 88.

[31]   Fraud against the poor was open-season. Political power was with the
Whigs, who were a combination of great landowners and new-money
men. 'The divine right of kings was replaced by the divine right of free-
holders' (Acton quoting Defoe in 'The History of Freedom in Christianity').

greater good by supplying both.[32] Lastly, English law was at
that time busy accommodating merchant law (the system of
international law known as *lex mercatoria*) into its system of
common law.[33] Merchant law concerned itself with regulating relations *between* merchants, and not with restraining
merchants on behalf of the general public. This last point is
significant for the legal status of bankers' privileges today.

The new form of banking was enormously profitable.[34]
By judiciously sharing a little of the profit among customers,
the new bankers attracted both depositors and borrowers.
Who would put gold in a strong-room that charged you to
store it, when close by someone else would pay you for the
privilege? Who would borrow from moneylenders at twelve
per cent, when you could borrow from bankers at six—or
even less?[35]

The new bankers lent claims to the government to finance its wars.[36] Charles II needed just such finance, not only
for wars but also for his court extravagances. A few years
later, in the 'Glorious Revolution' of 1688, Charles' successor
James II was ejected and a new King (William III) put in

---

[32]   These factors are reviewed in their contemporary context in Horsefield,
       British Monetary Experiments 1650-1710.
[33]   See 'General Survey Of The History Of The Law Merchant' by Thomas
       Edward Scrutton in *Select Essays in Anglo-American Legal History vol. 3*
       [1909]. Available online at Liberty Fund.
[34]   Before the development of English banking, Holland was the centre of
       world commerce. Soon, Dutch investment was pouring into England,
       and over the next century England replaced Holland as the centre of
       world commerce. Among the many reasons for Holland's decline,
       Charles Wilson identifies the lack of a central bank restraining the crea-
       tion of credit (see the relevant essays in his *Economic History and the His-
       torian*; also *England's Apprenticeship* (2nd ed. 1985, p 220). During the pe-
       riod 1650-1750 the Bank of Amsterdam, as Adam Smith relates, made it
       an object of pride to not lend what it did not have; but other, less scrupu-
       lous financiers were rampant.
[35]   See Sidney Homer, *A History of Interest Rates* (1977) pp 139-141.
[36]   Adam Smith gives an account of financing the Seven Years' war with
       bank-money which is all the more interesting because he has to resort to
       outright speculation, the dealings between governments and banks be-
       ing even more secretive then than they are today.

place—on the understanding that parliament was now the supreme power.

Parliament consisted of wealthy men elected by other wealthy men: their interests were commerce, capital and conquest. It seemed a good idea to the parliamentarians to incorporate bank-style money-manufacture for their own benefit and use. The Bank of England was established by Act of Parliament in 1694, initially to fund war-debt. From the very beginning, the Bank of England lent its capital at least twice over, to the government and to the public.[37]

The Bank of England and private banks created capital for borrowers and income for the government. The combination proved to be the engine-house of empire: wars could be waged, assets could be bought.[38] Capitalists could borrow almost any amount, provided bankers were convinced they could turn a profit. As for the government, it borrowed from bankers by promising future tax revenues to pay the interest. It could 'spend now, tax later'. Citizens and their children would have to foot the bill; or the debt would have to be financed from gains in foreign lands.

Military power and trade progressed hand-in-hand. Colonies were developed as profitable ventures: the slave trade burgeoned: Bristol and Liverpool became great cities on the back of it.[39] 'In the West Indies, the East Indies, and on the west coast of Africa, the age of exploration was everywhere giving way to the age of exploitation.'[40] The economy expanded fast, both at home and overseas, and despite the creation of large amounts of new money there was little inflation. The new banking system proved to be an excellent device for financing (and profiting from) empire.

---

[37] For a discreetly-put banker's version see Thorne F.W. *Banking* (1948) pp. 6-7; for a more direct economist's version, see J.K. Galbraith *Money: Whence It Came, Where It Went* p. 41

[38] Dickson, The Financial Revolution in England (1993).

[39] The Treaty of Utrecht (1713) which ended the War of the Spanish Succession gave England a near-monopoly of the slave-trade for thirty years (until the next war between Spain and England). For the financial importance of this see Hugh Thomas, *The Slave Trade* (1977) p. 235.

[40] Charles Wilson, *Profit and Power* (1957) p.111.

What were the domestic effects of this new money? Borrowers were able to purchase assets and labour, and to put them to work for profit. The government increased tax demands to pay interest on its growing 'national' debt. A heavy tax on land was introduced, which hurt small-to-middling landowners. In communities where few transactions involve money, demands for tax can only be met by contracting debt, and debt is often the back door to possession.[41] Many landowners borrowed to pay their taxes and then found they had to sell up—as often as not, to the bankers who had lent them money. An opposition member complained bitterly in parliament that taxes paid by small landowners went to create profit for bankers:

> The Landed Gentlemen bore the greatest Share of the [*burden of the*] Late War; by that they had been loaded with many heavy taxes: by that were all the Funds [*government debts*] created out of which the Plumb Men of the City of London have made most of their estates, by which they are enabled to deck their Wives in velvet and rich Brocades, while poor Country Gentlemen are hardly able to afford their Wives a Gown of Lindsey Woolsey.[42]

As for the poor, they were being dispossessed by other means: private acts of parliament (the 'Enclosure Acts', eventually amounting to over 3,000 in number) were taking away their livelihoods and rights in land.[43] Import taxes hurt them, as food became more expensive. Then (as now), the financial and commercial community could avoid many taxes: they were, after all, the majority power in parliament and in a position to set up and manipulate laws.[44]

---

[41] This is a trick both ancient and modern. Medieval monarchs had money-lenders always on hand to lend to people who could not pay their taxes.

[42] Joseph Bramber (1733) quoted in Dickson, *The Financial Revolution in England* (1993) p. 28. See also Charles Wilson, *England's Apprenticeship* (2nd ed. 1985) p 217.

[43] See Chapter 3 for details of this process.

[44] Whigs, who dominated the political scene, were 'associated with great interests in English society: with trade, and banking, and the city, with elements that were progressive, but exclusive, and devoted to private, not to national ends.' (Acton, 'The Rise of the Whigs' in *Lectures on Modern History*). When the legality and negotiability of banker's notes were

Landowners voiced their objections to the new bankers in terms that resonate today:

> A new interest has been created out of their fortunes, and a sort of property, which was not known twenty years ago, is now increased to be almost equal to the *terra firma* [land] of our island.[45]

Jonathan Swift, writing in 1713, observed the shift in power from land to finance.

> Artful men in Office and Credit [were able] to raise vast wealth for themselves in particular, who were to be the managers and directors in it… every new sum that was lent took away as much power from the landed men, as it added to theirs.[46]

Bolingbroke worried for the future:

> What will happen, when we have mortgaged and funded all we have to mortgage and fund… all the product of our land and even our land itself? Who can answer that the whole body of the people will suffer themselves to be treated as the poor Indians are in favour of the Spaniards, to be assigned to toil and starve… who can answer that such a scheme will always be endured?[47]

Such protests had little effect: the spirit and power of the times was against them. Then (as now) the virtues of 'progress' were loudly trumpeted by men with newly-created money: investment, management, productivity were the new virtues. The countryside and the cities filled with wandering and displaced poor, looking for employment or charity from those who had magicked away their assets.

The social consequences of bank-money, then as now, were most noticeable in the early days as banks, assisted by government demands for taxation, forced a transfer of assets

---

challenged successfully in the courts, parliament passed the Promissory Notes Act of 1704 making promissory notes of many sorts legal tender.

45 Henry St John (Bolingbroke) quoted in H.T. Dickinson *Liberty and Property* (1979) p. 52.

46 History of the Last Four Years of the Queen (pub. 1758) pp 130-1.

47 The Gentleman's Magazine, or The Monthly Intelligencer, Vol. 4. (1734).

on a grand scale from independent small producers to capitalists. The pattern observed here in England has been repeated all over the world.

It became apparent very quickly that the power of creating money could be dangerous for capitalists too if it was overused. Within thirty years of the foundation of the Bank of England two financial 'bubbles' grew and burst leaving financial devastation in their wake: the 'South Sea Bubble' in England and the 'Mississippi Bubble' in France (both in 1720). These bubbles left behind them a lesson: managed with restraint, privileged money-creation could be a source of great profit: unrestrained, it would lead to catastrophe. The lesson was not always remembered, of course, and there would subsequently be many hyperinflations and other crises such as the one we are living through today (2013); but it was there to be referred to.

World-wide legal accommodation of bankers' privilege copied its accommodation in English law, so it makes sense to look at how it was accommodated in England. The fundamental privilege, of owning deposits, was established not by public debate or in statute. After being practiced for some years, it was merely assumed to be part of 'the law of merchants' and therefore supported also in common law.

Circular arguments and ambiguous language hide what a bank actually 'is' in law. A banker is 'someone authorized to take deposits for the purpose of carrying on another regulated activity in accordance with that permission.'[48] In other words, banks are businesses which are authorized to behave as banks.[49] Eminent judges have protested (with no reaction

---

[48] *Commercial Law: Text, Cases and Materials.* Sealy and Hooley 2008, pp 610-11. Deposits taken by other businesses—for instance, by a shop from a customer who wants to reserve a TV set—remain the property of the customer and do not need to be regulated.

[49] Paget, *The Law of Banking* (1922, p.2): 'the custom of bankers, recognised in law, can only be formed and proved by legitimate bankers.' Abbott Payson Usher, on the other hand, declares straightforwardly that 'the essential function of a banking system is the creation of credit' (*op. cit.* p. 1). In European law, a bank is 'an undertaking whose business is to receive

from those who make laws). For instance, Lord Denning (1966): [50]

> Parliament has conferred many privileges on "banks" and "bankers", but it has never defined what is a "bank" or who is a "banker" It has said many times that a banker is someone who carries on the "business of banking", but it has never told us what is the business of banking.[51]

The 'democratic element' in this bizarre set-up seems to be: we authorize elected representatives, who authorize an authority to regulate banks, who operate a system set up by (and designed to favour) wealthy capitalists some three hundred years ago. Since the electorate and most representatives seem equally in the dark about what goes on, the democratic element is perhaps weak. Or is it non-existent?

If we want to know what banks are, we must look to the regulations to understand what they actually do. Banks are regulated in two ways vis-à-vis the creation of money. First, regulators limit the amount of loans banks are allowed to create relative to their cash: this is called the 'reserve ratio'. Second, regulators attempt to limit the extent to which banks expose themselves to the risk of bankruptcy: this it called the 'capital adequacy ratio'.[52]

So the privileges of banks insofar as they relate to the creation of money are: to treat other people's money as their own, and to lend the same money over and over again. These privileges exist 'by custom'. No popular debate surrounds their continued, almost hidden existence.

---

deposits or other repayable funds from the public and to grant credits for its own account'. 'Receiving deposits' and 'grant credits for their own account' are shamefully imprecise; indeed, they are misdescriptions.

[50] UDT v Kirkwood [1966] 2 QB 431 CA. The case can be read online at http://www.vanuatu.usp.ac.fj/courses/LA313_Commercial_Law/Cases/UDT_v_Kirkwood.html

[51] Denning actually repeats this point fourteen times, as if berating Parliament for its sinful omission.

[52] Although these two requirements overlap to a certain extent, both must be exercised in practice.

The courtroom scene referred to earlier gives a fascinating look into how the English judicial system accommodates banking in practice. Three judges in the English Court of Appeal are disagreeing over what makes a bank a bank. Two of the judges — Lords Diplock and Harman — are seemingly ignorant of what a bank actually does and are happy to recognise a bank as a business which 'accepts loans of money on deposit subject to withdrawal'. The third judge, Lord Denning, considers more widely the role of the law with regard to banks and commercial practice.

'When merchants have established a course of business which is running smoothly and well with no inconvenience or injustice,' he says, 'it is not for the judges to put a spoke in the wheel and bring it to a halt.' He quotes a long-standing legal principle 'from the time of Lord Coke'[53]: *communis error facit jus* — 'common error makes law'. A legal dictionary explains the principle: 'What was at first illegal, being repeated many times, is presumed to have acquired the force of usage, and then it would be wrong to depart from it.'[54]

This principle, says Lord Denning

> applies with especial force to commercial practice. When it has grown up and become established, the courts will overlook suggested defects and support it rather than throw it down. Thus it will enforce commercial credits, rather than hold them bad for want of consideration.[55] It is a maxim of English law to give effect to everything which appears to have been established for a considerable course of time and to presume that what has been done was done of right, and not in wrong.

Lord Denning states that one of the characteristics of bankers is that are 'at liberty to make use of the money' they hold on deposit. However, he does not list this as a privilege, merely as a characteristic. He then goes on to list twelve

---

[53]   Lord Coke, 1552-1634, called 'the greatest jurist of the Elizabethan and Jacobean eras' (Baker, 2002).

[54]   *A Law Dictionary, Adapted to the Constitution and Laws of the United States* by John Bouvier, 1856.

[55]   'Consideration' in this (legal) context means 'something had in return'.

privileges enshrined in statute.[56] They relate to secrecy, exemptions from liability, tax repayments, self-advertising and powers to expropriate. Privileges relating to money creation are not among the statutory privileges listed by Lord Denning: they are valid in law for the simple reason that they are customary practice. These practices are forbidden to others; therefore, it seems reasonable to call them 'unacknowledged privileges'.

The unacknowledged privileges of banks are supported in a similar manner in international law—as part of the customary practice of banks. Modern international commercial law has developed in international courts of arbitration.[57] Traders avoid using national legal systems, which tend to be slow, expensive, inexperienced in complex commercial transactions and in some countries corrupt. Traders tend to agree in their contracts that disputes arising should be resolved in one or other international court of arbitration (of which there are more than 150 with names such as ICC, LCIA, PRIME and SCC).[58] Courts of arbitration compete with each other (and with national law systems) for the lucrative business of providing satisfactory judgments for traders. National legal systems adapt to this new Merchant Law today just as English law adapted to the old Merchant Law in the 17th and 18th centuries.

The new Merchant Law conflicts in some respects with property law, just as did its medieval precedent. 'Many of

---

[56] Most of these are privileges of secrecy, allowing banks to hide the degree to which claims on their cash cannot possibly be met.

[57] For a summary see 'The new Lex Mercatoria and Transnational Governance' by Alec Stone Sweet in *Journal of European Public Policy* 13:5 August 2006: 627–646. Normally referred to as 'transnational commercial law', whether it deserves to be recognized as a separate legal system is disputed by, for instance, Professor R. Goode.

[58] 'This legal system—replete with its own 'a-national' law of contract and a system of private 'courts'—is parasitic on state authority. It uses state authority where necessary, essentially for enforcement purposes, while otherwise working to reduce the reach of sovereign control over transnational business… National legal systems, for their part, have steadily adapted to the Lex Mercatoria, thereby altering, among other things, the relationship between public and private power in Europe.' *Ibid.*

the rules of the Law Merchant were directed to evade inconvenient rules of the common law,' says a student textbook from 1929:

> One of the first rules of the common law is that a man cannot give what he himself has not. Consequently, when you buy a thing, if you are to be sure that you have title to it, you must inquire into the title of that thing back to its remote possessors, to make sure that no one in the chain of title stole it or obtained it by fraud. Whereas, the merchant said that commercial business 'cannot be carried on if we have to inquire into the title of everybody who comes to us with documents of title.'[59]

Banks, of course, lend 'what they themselves have not'. The privilege to do this is established in most countries by simple adaptation to Merchant Law.[60]

During the early days, English banking gave a tremendous advantage to English traders in their dealings abroad. They borrowed money easily and cheaply, and provided they turned enough of a profit they prospered. Later, during the nineteenth century, London became 'the place par excellence where both small- and large-scale borrowers from abroad could come for loans to develop their commercial projects and their countries.'[61] These foreign countries experienced the same shift in property relations—the same change from land-based to money-based elites—as England had experienced a century before.

For English bankers, foreign loans became a major source of income. 'International banks exist mainly to transfer capital in one form or another from countries where it is cheap to countries where it is dear.'[62] Bankers were proud their role in

---

[59] *A Student's Course On Legal History* (1929) by Helen West Bradlee. Cf. Holdsworth. The argument of traders depended on the principle of 'Market Overt': if transactions took place in open market and broad daylight, a buyer in good faith should obtain good title even to stolen goods.

[60] 'The legal orchestration of the privilege is clumsy,' writes Huerta de Soto, 'and usually takes the form of a simple administrative provision authorizing only bankers to maintain a reduced reserve ratio.' *Money, Bank Credit and Economic Cycles* (1998), p. 154.

[61] W.J. Thorne, *Banking* (1948) p. 30.

[62] A.S.J. Baster, *The International Banks* (Arno Press, NYT 1977) p. 1.

the expansion of Western power: 'by 1914 the great loan-issuing houses could not unjustly claim that it was largely by their efforts that Britain held in fee not only the Gorgeous East but the greater part of the rest of the world as well.'[63] This kind of expansion resumed on a large scale in the late 20th century, when ex-Communist countries put their assets up for sale and Western capitalists took advantage.[64]

Banking practice has changed a great deal over the years, but it still depends on the banker's magic trick of lending the same money again and again, in the process creating claims. The nature of the claims has changed: once they were gold-smith's receipts, next they were bankers' notes and cheques, now they are digits in deposit accounts.

Boom-and-bust cycles also continue with dreary regularity. They are less extreme than in the early days of the South Sea and Mississippi Bubbles, and they play out in slower motion. This suggests a question: are such cycles inevitable when money is created by banks? Logic would suggest they are.

Certain 18th century economists — Malthus, Ricardo, Sismondi[65] — pointed out an obvious fact: if all money ends up in the ownership of a few capitalists, and most people have no money to buy goods, then production will become unprofitable and must dry up. (Of course capitalists also con-

---

63   W.J. Thorne, *Banking* (1948) p. 31.

64   '[*In new member states of the EU*] nearly 70 per cent of banking assets are controlled by foreign banks, the percentage increases to over 80 per cent in the Czech Republic, Slovakia, Hungary, Estonia and Lithuania.' ECB report (2005) quoted in *Introduction to Banking* by Barbara Casu and Claudia Girardone, Philip Molyneux (2006).

65   For Malthus, see *Principles of Political Economy* (1836) Book Two, Chapter One, Section X. For Sismondi, see 'On the National Income, or the Income of the Community' (1835, tr. 1847). Ricardo points to ownership of the means of production as determining spending power: 'If machinery could do all the work that labour now does, there would be no demand for labour. Nobody would be entitled to consume anything who was not a capitalist, and who could not buy or hire a machine.' *Works* VIII, p 399. All are available free online at Liberty Fund.

sume and spend, but a single capitalist can only eat so many dinners, wear so many overcoats etc.).

As we have seen, bank-created money is a device invented for the purpose of transferring assets into the ownership of capitalists, a function it performs very well. As the proportion of bank-created money in the money supply increases, so this transfer of assets increases.

This transfer is evident in the day-to-day workings of banks. Claims — the money we use every day — disappear when a loan is repaid (see page 50). Meanwhile, interest payments continually transfer other claims (money) to bank ownership. Some of this bank income is used to pay running costs, and returns to circulation; some of it is invested, inflating asset (capital) prices; some of it returns to investors of capital, as profit. In other words, a proportion of interest payments transforms 'currency' — money used for spending — into 'capital' — money seeking investment. This augments the Malthus-Sismondi drift of currency to capital.[66]

So every bit of money created by banks as currency is created with two inbuilt mechanisms for its own destruction: either to disappear (when loans are repaid); or (via interest payments) to cease being currency and become capital. Both ways, it ceases to be money in circulation. This is the essential character of bank-created money, as distinct from money pure and simple.[67]

As the amount of currency diminishes, the system must go into crisis. There will simply not be enough money in circulation to pay for the goods and services that will make new loans profitable. Production cannot continue without a market: a market consists of customers both willing and able

---

[66] A generalised statement such as this can be easily disregarded or attacked. Because an economic event is the outcome of many different factors, economists disagree with each other simply by emphasizing a selection of factors. Mathematics is of limited use (beyond confusing the opposition) because it can only deal with a limited number of variables.

[67] The loans-to-deposits ratio of banks is significant here: whereas 20% was normal before 1945, 100% is now more usual, meaning that if all loans were repaid, all money in circulation (except notes-and-coins) would simply disappear!

to buy. Banks' appetites for making new loans must simply
dry up.[68] Only a massive drop in capital values, destruction
of capital assets, and/or new investment possibilities can re-
start the cycle. War is effective at the latter two of these.

The logic of this is both simple and congruent with what
happens. But although economists generally accept that
bank-created money exacerbates business cycles, there is
strong resistance to the idea that it actually causes them.[69]

The process outlined above, combined with government
taxation, borrowing and spending, causes a constant transfer
of assets from independently productive people to corporate
investors and government. It goes some way to explaining
the wealth gap in our present world, the recurring booms-
and-busts of the 'business cycle', and the need for relentless
growth to create new loans and new deposits for currency.

The distinction between cash and claims-on-cash seems odd
today when both are almost entirely digital numbers. Nevertheless, it is the system that banks and governments work to,
a carefully-nurtured continuation of the old system based on
gold and claims-on-gold which served them so well for so
many years.

The system needs growth to feed it: to keep the money
supply abundant. The rest of us may or may not care about
growth: we might feel fine if the size of the pie was constant,
or even a little smaller, but more equitably divided. We

---

[68]   Economics has proved remarkably resistant to the language and con-
cepts of cybernetics (the study of systems) which revolutionised most
practical sciences in the 20th century. For instance John Hicks, preferring
Newtonian descriptions based upon assumptions of equilibrium and
perfect competition, objected (*Value and Capital* 1939 p.84) that abandon-
ing these assumptions could lead 'to the wreckage of the greater part of
economic theory'. Since economics is largely a study of systems, the
wreckage might have been a prelude to better insight. Tyranny of theory
puts any discipline in danger of becoming an art of *ignoratio elenchi* –
elaborating the irrelevant.

[69]   Fisher, *100% Money* (1935); 'If some malevolent genius had sought to
aggravate the affliction of business and employment cycles, he could
hardly have done better than to establish a system of private deposit
banks in the present form' (p. 47).

might prefer reform of the banking system to the devastating effects of relentless growth. But we are not asked; indeed, we are generally ignorant of how banks create money and our ignorance is carefully nurtured and preserved.

As mentioned earlier, banks can create an infinite amount of money unless they come up against some restraint. Until thirty or so years ago, these restraints were more effective than they are today.

Two kinds of restraint act on the amount of money that banks create. First is the self-interest of banks and bankers. If they create too many claims on the same cash word gets round: people panic and claim 'their' cash. The bank then goes bust (it happened recently in Britain with Northern Rock) or demands an expensive bail-out.

The second kind of restraint is government regulation, which banks must accept as a condition of their license.[70]

Both kinds of restraint became dramatically less effective around the 1980's. First, the self-interest of individual bankers shifted like a weather-vane to an opposite direction, simply as a result of a change in how they were rewarded. While bankers were on a fixed salary it was in their interests that their bank should do well: it would survive and continue to pay them. Once they began to earn gigantic rewards from bonuses, however, it was in their self-interest to turn business over as quickly as possible, making loans regardless of whether they were good or bad for the bank. Bankers looted their own banks and retired rich: banks were placed on life-support, at citizens' expense.

The other form of restraint – by government regulators – was relaxed as politicians and central bankers became excited about the huge quantities of money being generated by unrestrained banking.

---

[70] This regulation is of two kinds. 'Reserve requirements' govern how many claims a bank may create on its cash: the ratio varies between 1 cash to 10 claims, and 1 cash to unlimited claims. 'Capital adequacy requirements' estimate the total worth of a bank and contrast it with how much the bank owes its depositors. The ratio has varied in recent years between 1 to 15 and 1 to 70.

Loss of restraint created a breeding ground for bizarre and outrageous financial instruments (derivatives and so forth, consisting essentially of claims-on-claims-on-claims etc., disguised by securitization). Mathematicians went to work to confuse and deceive innocent purchasers. Obscure legal principles were dug up to assist in fraudulent practice.[71] Outright corporate criminality also flourished and thefts of billions went unpunished.[72]

The scale and complexities of debt and temporary claims are now incomprehensible to the human mind. A 'shadow banking system', creating and trading complex financial instruments beyond regulation, feeds funds into the conventional banking system.[73] 'Quadrillion' is a fashionable new word for the amounts involved: if a pile of a million dollars comes up to a human knee, a quadrillion is high as a MILLION Empire State Buildings. Vast quantities of temporary 'money' expand and disappear like bubbles of gas, leaving behind real riches for some and real poverty for others.[74] Using the simple privileges of banks, the 'financial services industry' has become a gigantic predatory parasite draining the human and natural worlds of life.[75]

---

71   For instance the 'holder in due course' doctrine which 'is part of the little-known, often-ignored backwater that is negotiable instruments law and, simultaneously, is at the heart of today's great crisis of the American financial system, predatory lending.' Kurt Eggert, 'Held Up In Due Course', *Creighton Law Review*, Vol. 35 (2002).

72   Citigroup, MF Global, Goldman Sachs are some of the more public examples.

73   'The size of the balance sheet is no longer limited by the scale of opportunities to lend to companies or individuals in the real economy. So-called 'financial engineering' allows banks to manufacture additional assets without limit. And in the run-up to the crisis, they were aided and abetted in this endeavour by a host of vehicles and funds in the so-called shadow banking system, which in the US grew in gross terms to be larger than the traditional banking sector.' Mervyn King, Speech to the Buttonwood Gathering, New York, 25 October 2010.

74   David Ricardo: 'There is but one way in which an increase of money no matter how it be introduced into the society, can augment riches, viz at the expense of the wages of labour.' *Works*, 3, 319.

75   Goldman Sachs was described as 'a great vampire squid wrapped around the face of humanity, relentlessly jamming its blood funnel into

Where this scenario becomes extreme (in certain European states) ordinary citizens, bemused by the inertia and/or corruption of those who pretend to represent them, begin to imagine they would prefer the simplicity of one criminal, one organization, one set of rules however brutal, to a system in which they are helpless and uncomprehending victims. The spectre of totalitarianism rises once more.

The connivance of governments in perpetuating a system long past its sell-by date is at first sight puzzling. Is power so attractive, so intoxicating, that reason goes out of the window? Is ambition compatible only with shallow understanding? Is the prospect of reform too frightening? Do they believe that with a little tinkering we can carry on how we are?

Perhaps all of these: and there is more. Governments enjoy benefits from bank-created money which are available to them alone. They can borrow against the present and future work and wealth of their citizens without so much as a by-your-leave or a do-you-mind, to fund their expenditures.

Most debts are owed by or to a human person. The 'beneficial owner' of debt can be traced: if not an individual owner, perhaps a shareholder in a corporation. These owners can cash in or pay off their debts. Only the passive citizenry of governments are unable to opt in or out of the debts incurred in their names. The government holds them in an iron grip (unless they are rich enough to domicile elsewhere).

The bizarre element in this is that governments not only borrow in the names of their peoples, they simultaneously hold assets in the names of their peoples. An extreme example of this is the Chinese government which holds, in the name of its people, roughly 3 trillion in currency (earned from exports): it simultaneously owes its people getting on for three trillion in various types of debt.[76] Both these funds

---

anything that smells like money'. Matt Taibbi, 'The Great American Bubble Machine, *Rolling Stone*, April 5, 2010.

[76]   Debt owed at both national and provincial level. Official Chinese sources list the debt at 1.66 trillion: this excludes considerable assets held and

are available to it (and its favoured ones) for capital projects—and are most certainly not available to 'the people' in
whose name they are held.[77] The people cannot withdraw
from the contracts which bind them into lending and borrowing: the authority of the state in these matters is supreme. It is the same under all representative governments,
whether one-party as in China or multi-party as in the West.

Such funds enable governments to undertake not just
wars but immense financial and social projects. Arms production and sales worldwide are funded by money taken or
withheld from citizens, fuelling the competitive needs of
nations to bristle and sometimes fight.

What is perhaps even more important is that dependency
on the state and its projects—military, employment, welfare—transforms a nation in its collective mentality. There
will be more on this in chapter 6.

Meanwhile, the demands of debt grow until the prospect
of bankruptcy looms. 'Until World War I, no government in
history was able—even in wartime—to obtain from its people more than a very small fraction of its country's income—
perhaps 5 or 6 per cent,' wrote Peter Drucker.[78] Now, governments take nearer 50%.

Where governments take 50%, citizens must be doubly
productive to justify employment: their work must pay for
everything else. Employees in such states become uncompe-
titive. Corporations relocate production to where workers
are not so encumbered.[79] Unemployed workers become an
additional expense for the state: another vicious circle.

---

managed in the name of the people. *CIA World Handbook* (online) and
other sources.

[77]   Outside of the corporate entities known as 'governments' and 'peoples',
all debt and wealth can eventually be traced to some individual person's
ownership, even if only via a long chain of corporate ownerships.

[78]   *A Functioning Society* (2003) p. 60.

[79]   This was noted by Montesquieu: See *De l'Esprit des Lois*, Part 4 Book 22
Chapter 16.

The bankruptcy of governments, businesses and individuals is now so vast, however, that change is inevitable.[80] The question is: will change be intelligently managed, or will it take some extreme form? Privilege is often a prelude to revolution: it is generally a good idea to avoid revolution.

But, from where can we expect reform? None can be expected from international commercial law: contracts are supported as a matter of course, so long as no illegality is involved. 'Illegality' is defined by national legal systems, which conform anxiously to international practice, partly from convenience, partly to avoid exclusion from markets. Where can reform begin? Legal reform of banking privilege would inevitably isolate a nation from the international community. It would however be possible (in theory) for a nation to challenge banking privilege in the International Court of Justice.[81]

Over the centuries, objections have come from many quarters to banking privilege. Remarks made by United States presidents after leaving office are prominent among them. John Adams, for instance, second president of the United States, noted that bank-created money depreciated the currency: it also 'represented nothing, and is therefore a cheat upon somebody'; Thomas Jefferson, third president of the

---

[80] 'Zombies' is a new word for businesses, governments and individuals able to hang on to solvency only because interest rates are close to zero.

[81] The days seem remote when financial devices were examined in court for their benefit to the community as a whole, as for instance in debates over the value to society of the 'floating charge' (see Lord Macnaghten's judgement in the House of Lords in the case of *Salomon v Salomon*, 1897). As early as 1800, the commentator Edward Christian complained that merchant law had 'very unfortunately led merchants to suppose that all their crude and new-fangled fashions and devices immediately become the law of the land: a notion which, perhaps, has been too much encouraged by the courts (...) Merchants ought to take their law from the courts, and not the courts from the merchants; and when the law is found inconvenient for the purpose of extended commerce, application should be made to parliament for redress.' Edward Christian, quoted in *Readings On The History And System Of The Common Law* p. 223 (Roscoe Pound & Theodore F.T. Plucknett eds., 3rd ed. 1927).

United States, wrote that creation of money by banks would
'deliver our citizens, their property and their labour, pas-
sively to the swindling tricks of bankers and mountebank-
ers'.[82]

Adams' remark, that created money is a cheat upon
somebody, is surely spot-on: nothing comes from nothing,
and the value of created money is stolen from the value of
everyone else's money. Jefferson's remark was also pre-
scient. Over time, England, America, and other countries
that adopted the English system, found themselves transformed from nations of (predominantly) independent and
rightful occupiers into nations of (predominantly) dependent employees.

Vast cities of the poor and dispossessed bear testament to
this process today, and provide a cheap and needy work-
force for industries owned, either nominally or through debt,
by investors, banks and financial corporations.

We are now perhaps in a position to see who are winners
and who are losers in the game of money-creation.

The category of 'winners' is wide. Depositors and borrowers get better rates and charges. Managers take a lot in
salaries and bonuses, etc. Employees get paid; services and
buildings are paid for; governments receive taxes. Capitalists
are able to own more. A few entrepreneurs get started with
bank finance, although most have look to sources other than
banks.[83] Shareholders benefit from income and capital gains,
and not just shareholders: profits of ownership are re-
invested, inflating the value of capital assets generally, mak-

---

[82] 'Our medium is depreciated by the multitude of swindling banks, which
have emitted bank bills to an immense amount beyond the deposits of
gold and silver in their vaults, by which means the price of labor and
land and merchandise and produce is doubled, tripled, and quadrupled
in many instances. Every dollar of a bank bill that is issued beyond the
quantity of gold and silver in the vaults, represents nothing, and is therefore a cheat upon somebody.' Adams to Vanderkemp, 16 February,
1809. Jefferson's remark is in a letter to John Adams, March 21 1819.

[83] Usually because they have no collateral, people starting out in business
are not favoured by banks. They borrow from family, friends, associates.

ing everyone with assets a little richer.[84] Banks themselves inflate asset values by investing profits. They make available newly-created capital for speculation: this was responsible for the real estate bubble, as fund managers poured money into loans backed by homes.[85] By and large, winners are not primary producers, or if they are it is in some other area of their lives.

'Losers' include everyone who is out of the game or not successfully playing it. Some play incompetently; some do not want to play; some have no idea what the game is about. For most people, the game is something played far away in a place of which they have little or no knowledge. Their experience of the game is no fun at all: a slow loss of freedom and assets, punctuated with sudden traumas: homes and farms 'repossessed': a sinking into debt and a growing dependence on those who have filched their assets. By and large, losers are primary producers.

Most of all, however, the world loses what it could have been. Who can tell what kind of a world could have emerged, might still emerge, if capitalism was not privileged, but a level playing field: if it was fuelled by savings rather than by created credit. Who can even imagine a world in which governments are genuinely run by their peoples?

Electoral representation is now the dominant form of government across most of the world and it carries with it its characteristic system of banking. Late-coming nations find themselves robbed not only by powerful foreigners but also

---

[84]   'High real profits seem but modest returns to shareholders who have come in later and paid high prices for their stock (simply because dividends were high), not to the company but to the previous owners.' *The Economic Organisation of England'* Sir William Ashley, (1914), 1957, pp179-80. Averaging holding periods for US and UK bank shares fell from around three years in 1998 to around three months by 2008.' Andrew Haldane in *London Review of Books*, 23 Feb 2012.

[85]   'NINA' loans were made to people with 'No Income No Assets'; some loans were made to dead people. This jamboree led to the financial collapse of 2008. Summary: http://www.thisamericanlife.org/radio-archives/episode/355/transcript

by their own elites.[86] Once the robbing is done, elites may re-locate their assets to London or Miami or New York or to another centre of their choice, thereby further impoverishing their fellow-nationals and enriching their new home-country.

Money need not be created by banks. In *Monetary Experiments* Richard A. Lester demonstrated how money created equitably also stimulates economic growth.[87] In these conditions, lending and borrowing does not disappear: some people accumulate, save and have money to lend, others have projects and need to borrow. Straightforward money-lending is very different to the activities of banks, which create money in the process of lending it.[88] One can only wonder how the world would look today if enterprises had been funded from genuine savings, not from 'credit' created by banks — money based on debt.

Debt is a kind of servitude. Other freedoms lose their meaning if, desperate and anxious from debt, citizens live constricted lives amid the ravages of 'economic growth' whose main purpose, concealed under veils of pretence, is to increase the wealth of remote owners. The more remote the owners, the less knowledge they may have of how their wealth is being used, for good or bad.

How can this situation be changed for the better?

---

[86]   Western-style banking also greatly enhances opportunities for corruption. See, for instance, '$1bn fraud at Kabul Bank puts UK's Afghan pull-out in peril' *The Independent,* May 22, 2011 and 'Scandale étouffé à la Kabul Bank' in *Le Monde Diplomatique* 10/2011.

[87]   Richard A. Lester, *Monetary Experiments* (1939). Chapter V: 'Social Dividend in Maryland in 1733.'

[88]   In the 13th century Lombard bankers, by lending the same assets many times over, were able to charge low interest rates and thereby drove Jewish moneylenders out of the marketplace. This fact alone points out the devious psychopathology of writers such as J.A. Hobson, Ezra Pound, Henry Ford and my own grandfather Sir Oswald Mosley, who wrongly blamed banking on 'the Jews'. Banking was reinvented for the modern world by Lombards and established globally by nations following the English example. The Nazi banker Hjalmar Schacht was probably the most virtuosic banker of all time — in the service of the State (see below).

Every time the international and interconnected financial sector goes into crisis there is a flurry of discussion about reform. A battle of ideas takes place: on the one side are governments, banks and their dependents; on the other side are advocates of more sensible or fair ways of providing the money supply. So far, those against reform have always won. Eventually something has happened to kick off another boom—World War II, the collapse of communism, another revolution in production or technology—and thoughts of reform are (temporarily) forgotten.[89]

But after each crisis, a legacy of thought and writing is left behind by the defeated party for future consultation. The Great Depression—because it lasted so long—was particularly fertile for ideas, discussions, and suggested solutions.

Proposals for Reform

The object of this section is to outline a variety of proposals for reform that are currently being suggested.

To begin with, a suggestion for reform to be avoided: that is, nationalization of banking privilege. This suggestion is favoured by political extremists and is proving attractive to people in countries which have been bled dry by banks and investors. This could only lead in the direction of the totalitarian state.[90] The state would be able to pick up all the wealth and power which at present goes to banks and investors: suppression of freedom and democracy, mismanagement, and other monstrosities of twentieth-century totalitarianism would follow. The state, with its total power, would no doubt manage the trickle-down to consumers somewhat better, but at the cost of almost everything else.

---

[89] Einstein is supposed to have said, "I don't know what weapons World War III will be fought with, but World War IV will be fought with sticks and stones."

[90] Nazi state-sponsored 'Mefo bills' created claims-to-equity in the ratio of 12,000:1, giving huge purchasing power to the state. A special company was created with a million in capital; twelve billion was lent against it; the government bank exchanged these bills for money on demand. Banks have never come near to such an outrageous ratio: 60:1 is regarded as pushing it. See Avraham Barkai, *Nazi Economics* (1990) p 165.

Reform 1: No-privilege Banking

The basic idea of 'no-privilege banking' is simple: banks should obey the law like the rest of us. They should not be allowed to treat other people's money as their own; they should not be allowed to lend multiple claims on the same money; they should not be allowed to create money. What would 'no-privilege' banking look like? At the till end, for the average customer, it would not look hugely different. Banks would do what many people think they do: they would be safe-holders of deposits and intermediaries of credit.[91] Their services would be more expensive, but a great deal more affordable (for most) than the hidden price of banking today.

Customers would be asked (in a similar way to today): 'Do you want to be able to take money out whenever you like? Or would you rather leave it with us, say for five years, and we'll pay you some of the interest we get from lending it?' The bank would then marry up deposits and borrowers in a fairly simple fashion—and not lend out money which customers want to be able to access at any time.

Bank balance sheets would look quite different, more like those of ordinary businesses. Deposits would belong to depositors and not appear in the balance sheets. Inspection and accounting would be conducted with the aim of suppressing fraudulent practices, including those which aim to create money. Detected occurrences of fraud would lead to the same penalties as forgery, counterfeit and theft. In addition, as Henry C. Simons points out in proposals outlined later in this chapter, the types of property recognized in law would have to be simplified, to restrain the creation of financial instruments whose sole function is to increase the wealth of traders.[92]

---

[91]   Most reformers suggest also a separation of these two functions between different institutions, though if bankers had no privilege I doubt that would be necessary.

[92]   Simons, *Economics for a Free Society* p. 239. Chapter X: 'Debt Policy and Banking Policy'.

Amid the howls of outrage to be heard when such reforms are suggested is the protest: but there won't be enough credit for economies to flourish! Removing the privilege of banks to create money would indeed remove a certain kind of credit: the kind that is 'magicked' from the assets of others. Reformed banks, on the other hand, would be genuine intermediaries between would-be creditors and would-be debtors. Other ways of organising credit would become more competitive: true intermediaries such as friendly societies, credit rings, credit unions and mutuals, developed over the centuries, are with us still.[93] The market would presumably diversify: new sources of credit are now being developed, for instance by putting investors and entrepreneurs in touch with each other over the internet.[94]

There is also a fear that if banks in one country are not allowed to create money, that country will be vulnerable to banks which *can* create money—just as countries have been vulnerable in the past and are vulnerable today. That suggests an interesting question: what would become of a country that insisted upon its banks operating without privilege? Banks adopt the 'fractional reserve' system because it is more profitable: they would be fools not to.

An intriguing technical addendum: a bank compelled to maintain a 100% reserve ratio would (if integrated with the present banking system) swiftly gain cash from other banks via 'favourable clearing house balances'.[95] The presence of such a bank would (presumably) be intolerable to the system. At the moment, such an event is out of the question because banks act in tandem out of their own self-interest,

---

[93] An interesting case is the not-for-profit bank WIR, which, it is suggested, has contributed to Switzerland's relative economic stability during boom/bust crises. James Stodder, *Reciprocal Exchange Networks* (available online, March 2012).

[94] For instance, the Angel Investment Network and other 'angel' investment groups.

[95] See C.A. Phillips (1920) Chapters 3, 4 (particularly pp 77-8); also 'The Theory Of Multiple Expansion Of Deposits: What It Is And Whence It Came' by Thomas M. Humphrey, *Economic Review* March/April 1987 (available online at the Federal Bank of Richmond website).

expanding loans at the rate of what they can get away with, simply to maximize profit.

Reform 2: Governments and Currency Creation.

We are so familiar with money created as debt by banks that it is hard to imagine it being created any other way. Supposing money was created free-of-debt. Who would make it? How would it find its way into circulation?

When money circulated as coins — made of gold, silver and 'base metal' for the cheaper ones — the commonest complaint was that there was not enough of it. This didn't mean that people wanted to be given more money: it meant a shortage of coins in circulation was making it hard to exchange goods without resorting to barter.[96]

Coins entered circulation as payment. A merchant might take metal to the Mint because it would be worth more to him as coin than as metal: from that point on, coins drifted into circulation in payment for services, and circulated between people as a means of exchange. In other words, people were happy to 'buy' money in exchange for what they had to offer, because they knew they could use it to buy something else. The undisguised simplicity of this kind of economy, where money (valuable in itself) is swapped for something wanted by someone else, made it hard for individuals to amass vast quantities of money. Instead, power was gained and held by control of land and hereditary rights over others.

In the modern world, in so far as it is groping towards advances in democracy, neither type of power seems to be much of a good idea. There is no real democracy when most of the money (and therefore most of the power) is in the hands of privileged elites. 'No individual, no group, association or union can be entrusted with much power... it is mere foolishness to complain when absolute power is abused. It

---

[96]   In these conditions, money often became symbolic: an amount owing might be specified in currency but paid in another commodity, the amount being assessed by its known value in relation to coin. Again, see Usher: *The Early History of Deposit Banking in Mediterranean Europe.*

exists to be abused.'[97] It is also foolishness to believe that people with privilege will gladly give up their privilege — or support proposals to remove it. It is a rare person who, like Cincinnatus, voluntarily shuns privilege: elites have watched their worlds collapse around them rather than give up their privileges.[98]

Transitional periods are a concern: how would we move to a new banking order without the world collapsing around us? David Ricardo, suggesting reform of the Bank of England, proposed that money be created (by government) sufficient to make up the difference between the bank's cash and claims on its cash, and then given to the bank.[99] Variations on this idea have resurfaced (for instance on the Cobden Centre website).[100] Such a gift would not be inflationary, because the cash would stay put (be 'inert'). It would, however, shore up the property *status quo* and this might be undesirable, given the terrible poverty produced by years, decades and even centuries of filching.

Another possibility is to allow banks to go bankrupt, the government guaranteeing a certain minimum deposit (per individual, not per bank account!). Subsequently, banks would be authorised to reconstitute themselves, without debt, as true intermediaries of credit. Certain proposals already point in this direction, formulated by politicians in the event of catastrophic bank meltdown. When considering the consequences, an important consideration to bear in mind is that what most of us think of as 'money' is in fact debt, owed by banks to customers, which could not be repaid.

---

97 Oakeshott, 'The Political Economy of Freedom' in *Rationalism in Politics and Other Essays*.

98 One has only to think of the French Revolution or the collapse of Communism.

99 Ricardo was addressing the creation of money as bank notes. He denied that bank-credit creates money: see 'Evidence on the Resumption of Cash Payments' (1819, *Works*, Vol 5 p 437) and 'Plan For The Establishment Of A National Bank' (1823) Vol 4, pp 282, 283 (Liberty Fund Edition).

100 http://www.cobdencentre.org/2010/05/the-emperors-new-clothes-how-to-pay-off-the-national-debt-give-a-28-5-tax-cut/

Governments cannot be relied upon, however, while they are busy with their own deceits. Niall Ferguson observed in his 2012 Reith Lectures:

> The present system is, to put it bluntly, fraudulent. There are no regularly published and accurate official balance sheets. Huge liabilities are simply hidden from view. Not even the current income and expenditure statements can be relied upon in some countries. No legitimate business could possible carry on in this fashion. The last corporation to publish financial statements this misleading was Enron.

Reform 3: Corrective (Restorative) Justice.

From the time of Aristotle, an important part of justice has been 'corrective' or 'restorative' justice. The basic idea is pretty simple: when something has been stolen, it should be restored to its owner.[101] This has been known more recently as 'restitution' and a proper application of the laws of Unjust Enrichment would qualify a huge number of people for restitution.[102] This seems, however, a most unlikely outcome.[103]

However, it is still worth considering whether, given that much of the world's wealth has been transferred from independent owner-producers to creators of capital as a result of banking practice, some restorative justice is appropriate. Should the new property *status quo* just be accepted, or should there be an attempt to redress injustice? The situation is complicated by the fact that privileged money-creation, by and of its nature, has selected certain human qualities to prosper above others, and the qualities of our new elites are perhaps not of the best. Repudiations and negotiated reduc-

---

[101] 'The judge tries to restore equality by penalty, thereby taking from the gain.' Aristotle, *Nicomachean Ethics*, V, 4, paragraph 2. This has nothing to do with modern 'restorative justice' which involves trying to reconcile perpetrators and victims, and would be better called 'reconciliation'.

[102] *Unjust Enrichment* by Peter Birks (OUP, 2005). Chapter 1.

[103] St Augustine tells how Alexander the Great captured a pirate and took him to task for terrorizing the seas. The pirate replied 'because I do it with a little ship I am called a robber, while you, who do it with a great fleet, are styled emperor.'

tions of debt contain an element of restorative justice. At the moment, these happen only when they can no longer be avoided. Why should not banks go bust, and governments give set amounts of newly-created money to everyone? As for those now destitute, who were once just poor—should they be given assets to (for instance) re-purchase land or set up in business—or, for that matter, just to 'spend, spend, spend'?

In 1919 the economist John Maynard Keynes wrote of a world complicated by great debts, both internal and between nations, arising out of the First World War. Keynes recommended a carefully-conducted 'general bonfire' of debt. His advice was not taken. Twenty years later, war broke out in Europe once again. The debt situation today is not (so much) the result of war, but sentences from what he wrote ring bells for today: the passages that follow could hardly seem more apposite (the original is available online at Project Gutenberg, www.gutenberg.org):

> The policy of degrading the lives of millions of human beings, and of depriving whole nations of happiness should be abhorrent and detestable even if it were possible, even if it enriched ourselves, even if it did not sow the decay of the whole civilized life of Europe. A debtor nation does not love its creditor, and it is fruitless to expect feelings of goodwill if future development is stifled for many years to come. If, on the other hand, these great debts are forgiven, a stimulus will be given to the solidarity and true friendliness of nations.

> The existence of the debts is a menace to financial stability everywhere. There is no European country in which repudiation may not soon become an important political issue. In the case of internal debt there are interested parties on both sides, and the question is one of the internal distribution of wealth. With external debts this is not so, and the creditor nations may soon find their interest inconveniently bound up with the maintenance of a particular type of government or economic organization in the debtor countries. Entangling alliances or entangling leagues are nothing to the entanglements of cash owing.

> The final consideration influencing the reader's attitude must depend on his view as to the future place in the world's progress of the vast paper entanglements which are our legacy both

at home and abroad. We shall never be able to move again unless we can free our limbs from these paper shackles. A general bonfire is so great a necessity that unless we can make of it an orderly and good-tempered affair in which no serious injustice is done it will, when it comes at last, grow into a conflagration that may destroy much else as well.

As regards internal debt, I am one of those who believe that a capital levy for the extinction of debt is an absolute prerequisite of sound finance. But the continuance on a huge scale of indebtedness between Governments has special dangers of its own. Bankers are disposed to believe that a system between Governments, on a vast and definitely oppressive scale, represented by no real assets is natural and reasonable and in conformity with human nature.

I doubt this view of the world. Will the discontented peoples be willing so to order their lives that an appreciable part of their daily produce may be available to meet a foreign payment, the reason of which does not spring compellingly from their sense of justice or duty?'[104]

Reform 4: Money, Freedom and Democracy.

In relation to economics, the three qualities that we believe to be the foundation of modern civilization—democracy, freedom and equality—seem to genuinely share common ground. As mentioned before, debt is a kind of servitude. Destitution is worse: there is a pretty desperate kind of freedom in being broke, whatever the popular song may say.[105] Money only gives one kind of freedom, and perhaps corrupts others, but in the modern world it is a rare person who can live happily or well without it.

(i) Equitable distribution

Equitable distribution of new money—very different from equitable distribution of assets, because money quickly leaves some of us and just as surely is attracted to others—

---

[104] From 'The Economic Consequences of the Peace' by John Maynard Keynes (1919). Project Gutenberg, online.

[105] 'Freedom's just another word for nothing left to lose.' *Me & Bobby McGee*, Kristofferson & Foster.

would allow everyone at least a stab at equality of opportunity and it is certainly more democratic (by any definition of 'democracy') than current arrangements. Our modern affluence is mostly produced by machines. Sharing it would be more grown-up than fighting over it.

There exist historical examples of equitable distribution. For instance in Maryland, as told in *Monetary Experiments* by Richard Lester:

'When Maryland first issued paper money in 1733, most of it was given away — a certain sum to each inhabitant over 15 years of age.' This appears to have been 'the most successful paper money issued by any of the colonies... Hitherto, nearly all the people in the province had been engaged in the raising of tobacco... But now, wheat was raised, roads were cleared, bridges were built, towns sprang up, and facilities of social and commercial intercourse were thereby greatly increased.'[106]

A more modern story of equal distribution is told by R.A. Radford, of money emerging spontaneously in a specific currency in the confines of a prisoner-of-war camp during the Second World War.[107] Cigarettes were issued along with other goods in equal rations by the Red Cross. Cigarettes became the agreed currency, used by all inmates to value and pay for goods. As might be expected, some inmates became wealthy in cigarette-currency and others merely got by: wheeler-dealing, innovative business practices and smoking the currency all played their part in the redistribution of wealth. Debt in this situation is obviously unrelated to the issue of currency. From Radford's account, it would seem that debts were short-term and minor, contracted on the spot and soon redeemed.

---

[106] Richard A. Lester, *Monetary Experiments,* Princeton University Press (Reprinted David & Charles 1979) pp 142-151: he quotes from Gould, *Money and Transportation in Maryland, 1720-1765* (1915) and Mereness, *Maryland as a Proprietary Province* (1901).

[107] R.A. Radford, 'The Economic Organisation of a P.O.W. Camp' in *Economica* Nov. 1945.

Various suggestions that currency be distributed to all citizens, without either means test or work requirement, have come under the rubric 'basic income'. These payments would replace standard welfare payments and they would be paid to everyone whether or not they were in work. A 'basic income' is obviously a more equitable, and perhaps less toxic, way of distributing new money than present practice. It would also mean that wages would add to, rather than replace, state-supplied income, thereby eliminating the 'poverty trap'. A surprising variety of people have supported this idea under the name Guaranteed Annual Income (for instance US Presidents Nixon and Carter).[108] Whether new money would be distributed as and when monetary stability requires, or whether some steady and guaranteed amount would be supplied, would be the key consideration here.

These kinds of innovation have been relentlessly (and so far victoriously) opposed, not just by self-interested beneficiaries of government and business, but also by a strong puritanical element in Western civilization which views the poor as unruly, undeserving, improvident and a variety of other epithets used to justify what historian Preserved Smith has called the 'ceaseless war on the poor'.[109] Even when governments create money, there seems to be a reluctance to let it enter circulation outside the control of banks.[110] Is there a fear of the poor regaining their independence? Do the affluent believe that affluence is theirs by moral right? To this,

---

[108] See Brian Steensland, *The Failed Welfare Revolution: America's Struggle Over Guaranteed Income Policy*. Princetown University Press, 2008.

[109] Preserved Smith, *The Reformation*. The chapter on 'The Rise of the Money Power' is as interesting as Weber's famous book on the same theme, *The Protestant Ethic and the Spirit of Capitalism* (1905).

[110] Keynes apparently thought that new money should be hidden buried in milk-bottles so that only needy people, who would actually spend it, would bother looking for it. 'Quantitative Easing' is the opposite of this practice: feeding cash in at the top end in the hope that it will be multiply lent.

Acton remarked, 'there is not a more perilous or immoral habit of mind than the sanctifying of success.'[111]

(ii) A Return to Commodity Money

The origins of money are lost in pre-history. Archaeologists tell us that commodities such as gold, cowry shells, salt, rice and cattle were in use as currencies long before written records. These commodities were valuable in themselves: gold and shells were valued as jewellery and ornaments; copper for its use in making vessels; salt, rice and cattle for food. For thousands of years, money continued to be made of something valued in its own right—most usually of metals, because they can be easily shaped into different sizes and weights. This kind of money is now referred to as 'commodity money'. It cannot be created out of nothing and its value as money tends to stay pretty close to the value of what it is made of.

Many of these commodities were used as money with no alteration. Metals were of course transformed when made into coin, but we have seen how there were not usually huge profits in the process. The relative stability of money continued with paper money, for as long as each piece of paper represented a piece of gold or silver in storage.[112] As we saw earlier with the 'goldsmith bankers', it was only when paper claims began to be issued in excess of stored bullion that rampant money-creation began, resulting in great riches for some and gradually increasing poverty for others.

Seeking a return to stability, many suggestions for reform centre on a return to a gold standard, or to currencies fully

---

[111] Acton, *Lectures in Modern History: The Puritan Revolution*. The connections between Protestantism and capitalism are explored in a number of classics (Weber, Tawney). Puritans tell us that God sanctified capitalism in the Parable of the Talents (Matthew, Ch. 25) but it contains no mention of multiple lending. Christians might also note the Parable of the Unjust Steward, where a servant is praised for currying favour with his master's debtors by letting them off (Luke, Ch. 16).

[112] This was the system recommended by David Ricardo; it would now be called 100% reserve.

backed by stored precious metals.[113] A related suggestion is
that everyone should have the freedom to create currency, so
long as it is backed by stored precious metal.[114] There are,
however, great inequities and complications in systems
based on precious metal which in any case now seem redundant, as if we were all to go back to travelling on horses
or to dispense altogether with reading and writing.[115]

<u>(iii) Fiat Money</u>

Most of what the law recognizes as 'money' today is mere
information stored in computer systems. Only a small proportion (3% is the figure usually quoted) of pounds, dollars,
etcetera, is made of paper or metal coin, and that too is
cheaply produced.[116] When the purchasing power of money
bears no relation to what it is made of, it is called 'fiat
money' (*fiat* is Latin for 'Let it be done!'). It is acceptable as
money by state decree.[117]

The challenge is surely to manage 'fiat' money in a way
which is transparent, equitable, and comprehensible to anyone who cares to take an interest. In other words, in a way
exactly opposite to the way it is done at present (opaque,
inequitable, and incomprehensible finally even to those who
are managing it). The design would be capitalistic in that

---

[113] These suggestions are thoroughly explored on The Cobden Centre website. Ricardo's preferred option was 100% gold reserve. Ron Paul stands
repeatedly for Republican presidential nominee on this ticket.

[114] The idea is discussed critically by James Tobin: 'Financial Innovation
and Deregulation in Perspective', in *Monetary and Economic Studies* (Bank
of Japan) Vol 3, Issue 2, Sept 1985.

[115] The worst being, perhaps, the wars that were fought over gold, just as
they are fought over oil today.

[116] Paper and coin are manufactured by governments and sold by them to
banks. 'The cash is exchanged at face value for an equal amount of electronic central bank money taken from the BoE reserve account of the re-
questing bank, or sometimes for gilt stock owned by the bank. The
commercial bank exchanges one asset for another.'
www.positivemoney.org.uk

[117] When 'real' money was gold or silver coin, notes were merely claims on
real money. Now, however, they are valued for their regulated scarcity
and legally-sanctioned acceptability as a means of payment, not as
claims on coin. They are cash.

saving and lending would play their part; but the playing field would be level, not tilted towards capital, thereby restoring some meaning to the phrase 'free-market economy'. Savings, rather than 'created credit', would be lent. Deposits would consist of real money, not claims created in the act of lending.

The great advantages of fiat money—easy and almost cost-free production, and independence of a particular commodity such as gold—also give rise to its main drawback, which is that vast amounts can be created merely by printing, or pressing computer keys. When governments do this, hyperinflation is the result. When bankers' privilege does it, the result is legalised misappropriation. When both do it together, the human and natural worlds are ravaged to and beyond the limits of their endurance.

Fiat money works, no doubt about that: most currencies in the world today consist of it. Problems arise from abuse of the system, not from the system itself. Given that it is so easy to abuse, is it foolish to imagine it ever might not be abused?

One suggestion is that no new money should be created beyond what is already in circulation.[118] This would mean money varying in value as quantities of goods, expectations, appetites, etcetera, grow or shrink. If the smallest unit of currency became almost worthless, it could be abandoned; if it became too valuable, a new smaller unit could be introduced. If this policy were adopted, then money creation by financial institutions would be made a distinct crime and money creation by governments constitutionally abandoned. The problem with this is that money would be always changing in value. Inflation and deflation, with their many attendant problems, would become the order of the day.[119]

If, on the other hand, stability in purchasing power (money keeping a steady value) is to be aimed at, money has

---

[118] '...changes in money demand can always be met by changes in money's purchasing power'. Detlev Schlichter, *Paper Money Collapse* (2011), p.33.

[119] For the advantages of monetary stability see *Lectures On Economic Principles* by Dennis Robertson, Vol III pp31ff.

to be sometimes created and sometimes destroyed. If banks were no longer allowed to do this, who would do it?

Government (through their treasury departments and central banks) attempt to manipulate how much money is created by banks. If banks were no longer allowed to create money, this role would be redundant. If the task of money creation was to be associated with 'government' how should it be instituted, controlled, and made accountable?

Two of the best-known economists who have advocated government control of the money supply—Ricardo and Simons—were well aware of how badly governments like to behave. They both advocated the formation of a separate agency for providing a stable currency, effectively a fourth power adding to the existing three of executive, legislative and judiciary.[120]

It is surely true that control of the money supply, like the justice system, should be a power separate from the legislature and the executive. Entrusting it to legislatures and banks has been a disaster. Like the justice system, it should be both open to scrutiny and contain a true democratic presence: juries selected by lot, considering at length and actually making decisions.

When governments create money for their own use, it amounts to another form of taxation: the currency loses value and everyone gets poorer.[121] Governments commandeer resources for a vast array of activity: wars, welfare, health, roads, social services, diplomacy, education, police, standing armies, and so on and so on. Some government expenditure is undertaken for agreed common benefits, some to buy votes in the next election, some to attempt to engineer us into more compliant citizens. Each of these activities is (and should be) subject to argument as to whether

---

120 For Ricardo see 'Plan For The Establishment Of A National Bank' (1823) in *Works* Vol 4 (Liberty Fund Edition). For Simons, see later in this chapter.

121 Because it takes a little from everyone in proportion to how much they have, it could be a genuinely progressive tax—except that money can be moved between currencies, so it would also be an easy tax to avoid.

it is appropriate, efficiently conducted, better left to others or better not done at all: but money for these projects should not be raised surreptitiously. We should always bear in mind the economist Bastiat's humorous epigram: 'The state is the great fictitious entity by which everyone seeks to live at the expense of everyone else.'[122]

Questions of how government should spend our money are different to the simple question: How much money should be created or destroyed, purely to aim at a steady value for money? A separate power would protect that difference.

How would people be chosen to make up this separate power? Not from political parties, who are partisan by nature and inclined to offer other people's money to their constituents. Nor should they be selected from the establishment, which tends to favour itself. Only a totality of the people can be expected to guard against privilege for one part of it. A jury selected from *all* the people is the obvious answer, tried and tested over centuries in courts of law (see Chapter 7, below). Just as in trials by jury, presentations could be made by experts and interested parties, and summings-up given by a competent adjudicator before decision by vote from the jury. For such an important duty the jury could consist of many hundreds of people.

There is, however, an addendum to the rule that the totality of a people can be relied on to outlaw privilege, which is that an entire people may (and often does) enjoy privilege over another people. Just as electoral representation may produce oppression by one class over another, so (true) democracy may produce oppression by one nation over another.[123] The Athenians and the Swiss, both notably and

---

122   *L'État* (1848).

123   Acton: 'the tyranny of the majority, or rather of that party, not always the majority, that succeeds, by force or fraud, in carrying elections' ('The History of Freedom in Antiquity', 1877.) For examples, see Chapter 5.

truly democratic at home, were notoriously oppressive abroad.[124]

This is a good reason why banking should be (as it is to some extent already) governed by global agreements. The change needed is for legislation and regulation to be made with popular knowledge and consent, rather than administered by those who stand to benefit.

During the Great Depression (roughly 1929-39) Henry C. Simons recommended a careful strategy for moving towards a healthy banking and monetary system. Government policy, then as now, was struggling to stimulate economic recovery without reforming the privileges of banks. Goods were being manufactured in huge amounts, but ordinary people did not have money to buy them. Then as now, banks were popularly blamed, but supported by anxious governments. Then as now, the idea of creating money equitably was anathema to the powerful.

Being realistic about the corrupt tendencies of governments, Simons suggested that money creation should involve scrutiny and deliberation by the people.[125]

The authority responsible, Simons wrote, should have 'a direct and inescapable responsibility for controlling (not with broad discretionary powers but under simple, definite rules laid down in legislation) the quantity (or through quantity, the value) of effective money.'[126] The rules should be not just simple but 'expressive of strong, abiding, pervasive and reasonable popular sentiments'[127] so that the public would take an interest in what was going on and exert moral pressure against 'administrative and executive tinkering.' The authority would be a separate power within the state. It

---

[124] See Benjamin Barber, *The Death of Communal Liberty: A History of Freedom in a Swiss Mountain Canton*. Princeton University Press, 1974. Pp. 148-156. The Swiss episode was the Graubunden domination of the Valtellina in the 16th–18th Centuries. The most famous act of imperial barbarity by democratic Athens was its extermination of the Melians (416 BC).

[125] Henry C. Simons, *Economic Policy for a Free Society*. University of Chicago Press, 1948, pp. 181-2.

[126] Simons, *Economic Policy for a Free Society*, pp. 57, 181-3.

[127] Simons, *Economic Policy for a Free Society*, p.181.

would operate with the sole objective of pursuing stability in prices by adding to, or subtracting from, the money supply.

The process would not be complicated. If there is too much money in the system, Simons said, the authority would instruct the government to increase taxes and put money into cold storage; if there is not enough money, the government would be authorized to create money and spend it.[128] Since today (2013) governments habitually spend between thirty and fifty per cent of GDP, there would be plenty of room for manoeuvre. Approval of what the government spends its money on would be a separate issue governed by political mechanisms already in place.

Simons thought that suppression of private money creation would unavoidably be subject to some disappointments because the ingenuity of tricksters would keep them one step ahead of the law.[129] However, with genuinely democratic supervision there would be a strong chance that new abuses would be detected and stopped.

To further pre-empt the ingenuity of tricksters, Simons recommended reform of property law, so that layers-upon-layers of claims could not be used to generate money and hide other types of fraud.[130] This would also do away with unauthorised contracts between financial operators based on money and claims owned by others (thereby conflicting with basic principles of property law, even while conforming to commercial practice).[131]

---

[128] Or as Simons puts it, in the language of economese: 'The powers of the government to inject purchasing power through expenditure and to withdraw it through taxation — the powers of expanding and contracting issues of actual currency and other obligations more or less serviceable as money — are surely adequate to price-level control.' *Economics for a Free Society*, p. 175. The fact that most money now consists of electronically recorded numbers (as opposed to metal or paper) makes little difference; it is still money.

[129] 'the reappearance of prohibited practices in new and unprohibited forms'. p. 172.

[130] Simons, *Economic Policy for a Free Society*, p. 38.

[131] Buying-and-selling contracts are not valid if they involve property rights unrecognized in law: I, for instance, cannot sell the British Navy.

The two traditional roles of high street banks should be separated, Simons said. Banks should be of two types: one which accepts, stores, and transfers actual currency; another which provides long-term lending of actual assets.[132] This would make fraudulent money-creation harder to conceal.

To restrain financial corporations from inventing new methods of 'money-bootlegging', he suggested simple reforms of the borrowing powers of corporations 'to prevent their effectively taking over the prerogatives of which banking corporations as such had been deprived.'

'If such reforms seem fantastic, it may be pointed out that, in practice, they would require merely drastic limitation on the powers of corporations (which is eminently desirable on other, and equally important, grounds as well).[133]

Simons wrote for the benefit of other economists, believing he could influence them through argument and that they in turn would influence the course of political events. One by one, however, his colleagues accepted salaries from business or government and fell silent on the subject of privileged banking. Simons committed suicide in 1946. Meanwhile the Great Depression fizzled out in the vast capital destructions of World War Two.

Can we improve on the kind of program suggested by Henry C. Simons? Are his proposals as 'fantastic' as he thought? The separation of retail and investment banking has once again become the focus of government policy on both sides of the Atlantic. For the U.K. the creation of the non-political Monetary Policy Committee (1997) might one day seem, in retrospect, the first step towards the kind of independent authority Simons proposed. The vital ingredients are still missing, however: acknowledgement of, and public familiarity with what is going on, and a truly democratic procedure capable of eradicating privilege.

It is hard to imagine that a jury of ordinary people, after careful deliberation, would allow banks to create 97% plus of new money as debts to and from themselves.

---

132 Simons, *Economic Policy for a Free Society*, p.171.
133 Simons, *Economic Policy for a Free Society*, p. 171.

Chapter Five

Representative Government II: The Export Model

Previous chapters have looked at electoral representation as a home-grown product in England, France and the USA. Despite the rhetoric, its performance as a form of government has not been very 'democratic' if by democracy we mean 'rule by the people'. Has electoral representation proved more democratic as an export?

The myth that electoral representation is democratic is certainly a powerful one. Again and again, it inspires people held in the grip of tyranny to armed rebellion. This is hardly surprising, given that rule by a tyrant tends to be the worst form of government in the world. The freedom to vote out murderers, torturers and corrupt politicians must seem like a vision of heaven to those caught in tyranny. But do elections deliver democracy?

Electoral representation as an export model shares many characteristics of the home-grown variety; but it tends to arrive more suddenly and some of its characteristics get highlighted in the process.

The divisive nature of electoral representation is one of these characteristics. Political parties represent interest groups and set them one against the other. Elections offer the hope that one will be able to dominate the rest. In a very diverse society, there may be no particular separation of interest groups along lines of religion, class or race. But in nations stratified across clear divisions, party alignment may be dramatically racist, sectarian or class-based. In the 2009 election in Iran, for instance, the middle classes voted one way, the poor another: the candidate of the poor won (and the world took fright).

In more extreme cases secession, civil war, or even genocide has been the outcome of divisive party politics. Germany transferred sovereignty to its elected assembly in 1919. In elections of 1932 and 1933 the Nazi party won more votes than any other party on a racist agenda: what followed is the best-known sequence of events in modern history and the worst disaster to befall the human race so far.

In Yugoslavia, the communist dictator Tito held together a country with several languages and religions: once he was gone, the country adopted electoral representation and sectarian parties struggled for votes by inciting civil hatreds and genocidal crimes.

In Rwanda, Tutsi domination was no longer sustainable after multi-party electoral representation was adopted in 1961. With Hutus at almost 80% of the population, power became a matter for internal struggle within the Hutu: factions competed for votes using ethnic rhetoric against the Tutsi, culminating in the genocide of 1994.

The record of electoral representation with regard to genocide is generally not good. There are many other sequences of events to ponder on, beginning with what has been called (controversially) the first European genocide—in the Vendée—perpetrated by Europe's first purely elected government in 1794. In Turkey, multi-party elections were first held in 1908: the winning party promoted the genocide of Armenians and other minorities in 1915.[1] Sudan held its first elections in 1953: genocidal civil war began in 1955. Britain and the United States both engaged in what are now considered by many to be genocides during their early peri-

---

[1] *The Revolution of 1908 in Turkey* by Aykut Kansu (1997). A popular assembly had been elected earlier, in 1876 (the Meclis-i Umumi), but it never enjoyed 'real power vis-à-vis the monarchy and the bureaucracy' (p. 2).

ods of government by elected representatives (against Native Americans, Irish, Australian aboriginals). During the partition between India and Pakistan (1947) roughly a million Muslims and Hindus were killed fleeing the prospect of elective government dominated by the other side.

In his classic text on the subject (in which he uses the word 'democracy' to mean multi-party electoral representation) Michael Mann stresses that genocides have happened throughout history: 'We will not find any simple overall relationship in the world today between democracy and ethnic cleansing'.[2] But (representational) democracy 'has always carried with it the possibility that the majority might tyrannize minorities, and this possibility carries more ominous consequences in certain types of multiethnic environments.'

Mann sees genocide as an early-stage feature in government by electoral representation. Later, things settle down and become what political theorists call 'mature democracies'. Michael Mann:

> Stably institutionalized democracies are less likely than either democratizing or authoritarian regimes to commit murderous cleansing. They have entrenched not only elections and rule by the majority, but also constitutional guarantees for minorities. But their past was not so virtuous. Most of them committed sufficient ethnic cleansing to produce an essentially mono-ethnic citizen body in the present. In their past, cleansing and democratization proceeded hand in hand. Liberal democracies were built on top of ethnic cleansing, though outside of the colonies this took the form of institutionalized coercion, not mass murder.

This would suggest that genocide has been a kind of original sin in what are called 'representative democracies'.[3]

In another acclaimed book on the subject, Amy Chua stresses the vulnerability of wealthy minorities to state-

---

[2] Michael Mann, The Dark Side of Democracy: Explaining Ethnic Cleansing (2004).

[3] Later, a new ethic appears to arrive concerning ethnic minorities, with a need on the one hand for immigrant labour and on the other for immigrants of extreme wealth.

sponsored attack under elected governments, mentioning the Jews in Nazi Germany, the Chinese in South-East Asia, the Lebanese in West Africa, all of whom have suffered genocidal assaults; also the Tamils in Sri Lanka, and tribes which have constituted traditional ruling classes in Africa.[4]

Blaming 'democracy' for such events, however, is like blaming an innocent person for the crimes of an impostor. Societies with a measure of true democracy — ancient Athens, the colonial government of Rhode Island, modern Switzerland — have not embarked on the extermination of domestic minorities (whatever else their crimes). On the contrary, their political orders were specifically built around avoiding internal strife.[5] They are integrative rather than divisive.

Athens was built on the coming together of several tribes (*synoecism*): Cleisthenes, the architect of democracy, divided and re-classified Athenian citizens in order to avoid tribal factionalism.

The early American colony of Rhode Island designed its constitution democratically (1644, 1647, 1663) to avoid religious violence, which it left behind in Europe but was still raging in neighbouring colonies. It bought land from the Native Americans (instead of taking it) and had good relations with them, until war between settlers and natives in neighbouring Massachusetts and Connecticut poisoned relations.

Switzerland is composed of three distinct ethnic groups speaking four different first languages; it tolerates many religious sects and incorporates many different political traditions: it has lived mostly in domestic peace and prosperity for centuries.[6]

---

4   Amy Chua, *The World on Fire* (2003).
5   Wolf Linder's book *Swiss Democracy* (1994) is subtitled 'Possible Solutions To Conflict In Multicultural Societies'.
6   In 1847, Switzerland had a short civil war. Casualties were so few (less than a hundred dead) that Bismarck described it contemptuously as a 'rabbit-shoot'. See James McPherson, *A Very Civil War: the Swiss Sonderbund War of 1847* (1993).

A second feature of electoral representation highlighted in the 'export model' is that it opens up a country to appropriation by new elites. The prediction made by Maitland over a hundred years ago—that unless electorates concerned themselves with knowledge of the law, it would be used to their disadvantage—is a ghost that has stalked the world ever since. Citizens have proved easy meat for robbery by elites, both foreign and home-grown.[7]

Creation of capital by Western banks was described in Chapter Four. With this cheaply-created money, Western investors have been able to buy the assets of 'emerging' countries as they integrate with Western systems of banking and finance. After the Second World War, opportunities presented themselves in two phases: first, the disintegrating empires of the West (British, French, Portuguese, Dutch); then the collapse of the Soviet empire.

As colonies won their freedom, old colonial powers were keen to maintain their profitable access to markets and raw materials. Newly elected governments in the colonies were tempted by lucrative contracts into granting licenses. This developed into a simple formula: a supply of money and guns to governments (most of which then abolished elections) in exchange for access to raw materials. As a further corruption, money received 'in the name of the people' often went straight into the bank account of a government minister, the account invariably being with a Western bank.

For many countries, from colonialism to post-colonialism was a case of 'out the frying pan, into the fire'. After voting once, people were held in check by machine-guns while their gangster governments, sponsored by outside powers, robbed, terrorized and murdered them. This kind of business proceeded, and proceeds still in many countries today, with the full knowledge of Western powers. Little was done for many decades by the West to restrain their part in it.

---

[7] From one of the last poems of Edwin Muir, *Ballad of Everyman*: 'Curses upon the traitorous men / Who brought our good friend everyman down / And murder peace to bring their peace / And flatter and rob the ignorant clown.'

As for countries emerging from communism, Western banks struck deals with party bigwigs. Assets owned nominally by 'the people' were sold off cheaply. Profits were shared between banks, investors and ex-party apparatchiks — who, suddenly rich, became the country's new elites.

As if corporate banks were not bad enough for the world, international institutions were set up to manage the provision and payback of created debt: the World Bank, the International Monetary Fund and a variety of Credit Export Agencies (whose business is to lend in conditions of secrecy).[8] Locals could not compete: to begin with at least, they had not the contacts, the experience, the institutions or the collateral needed to borrow.

The United States of America has been the dominating power in the West since the end of the Second World War and it has used that power both openly and covertly to influence domestic politics in other countries.

It is, of course, possible to believe absolutely that the U.S is the champion of freedom and democracy. Once that veil of belief is drawn back, however, possibilities of understanding our contemporary world open up considerably.

Bearing in mind the number of terrible dictatorships the U.S. has supported and the fact that foreign elections are regularly overturned by U.S. actions (both open and covert) when they produce the 'wrong' outcome, it seems appropriate to seek to a more complex understanding of U.S. forays into world affairs.

Whether one reads an account by a disappointed conservative such as George Kennan,[9] factual narratives such as those by Stephen Kinzer,[10] or passionate radical accounts such as those of William Blum,[11] the impression gained is of

---

8   See Bruce Rich, 'Exporting Destruction' in Steven Hiatt, ed., *A Game As Old As Empire* (2007).

9   *American Diplomacy* (expanded edition, 2012).

10   *Overthrow* (2007).

11   *Rogue Nation* (2002), *Killing Hope* (1998). Due for publication January 2013: *America's Deadliest Export – Democracy*.

a wide gap between the 'noble postures'[12] of American politics and its true motivations, let alone its results.

For outside observers, the great puzzle of the United States is that gap and the public culture which allows it. The exclusion of intelligent humanitarian voices from policy, and increasingly from the marketplace of public opinion, has been a tragedy for the world as well as for America.[13]

Long before the Second World War, the United States was overturning foreign governments in pursuit of its imperial and/or commercial interests. In 1898 America went to war with Spain using business interests as an excuse, even though most business lobbyists were against the war.[14]

The new, partially hidden empire of American interests was confronted by a problem common to all empires. Should foreign policy encourage the independent manufacturing and trading capacity of foreign countries, reinforcing their strength and independence as allies? Or should policy be to dominate, undermine and exploit, always seeking one-sided gain?

It seems that the latter principle, victorious in 1898, was never seriously challenged in the corridors of power. The American empire likes to act as if it were no empire: reluctant to take and administer territory, it attempts both openly and in secret (and not always successfully) to manipulate events to its own advantage.[15]

The relevant question for U.S. foreign policy, vis-à-vis the domestic politics of other nations, became in effect: what form of government in a such-and-such a country would prove most lucrative for what were called 'U.S. interests' — the interests of their plutocrats?

---

[12] George Kennan's phrase: *American Diplomacy* (2012 edition) p 180.

[13] American public opinion is in general remarkably tolerant of its government promoting murder, torture, destabilization and civil violence abroad. The 'moral majority' is silent: it is left to radicals to be outraged.

[14] Julius W. Pratt: 'American Business and the Spanish-American War' in *American Imperialism in 1898* (1955).

[15] The historic reasons for this are traditionally given as the anti-imperial, anti-monarchical origins of the U.S. which makes it reluctant to see itself as now an empire.

Policy unfolded into two different directions, depending upon a country's economic development. If a country was prosperous enough—if the opportunities of its markets were judged to outweigh the lure of its natural resources—it would be encouraged into elections, in the knowledge that representative government would provide the best access to its markets. If the wrong party was elected, matters could be taken in hand by destabilization, deposition and/or murder.[16] If access to raw materials was judged to be the most important consideration, a client dictator would be the best option ('He may be a son-of-a-bitch but he's our son-of-a-bitch' is a quote attributed to many U.S. presidents since Abraham Lincoln.)[17]

The client dictatorships which resulted have been some of the most horrible governments in the history of humanity, and a testament for all time that covert empires can be a great deal worse than open ones.

'America' was not the beneficiary of its foreign policy if by 'America' we mean the people of America. The beneficiaries were the powers of corporate business—the same powers which were simultaneously profiting from moving factories abroad and indebting American citizens.[18]

Bit-by-bit the immense goodwill of the world towards America was squandered. The independence and moral freedom of its citizens was also corroded, as the obligation to 'support one's country right or wrong' superseded real and traditional virtues.[19]

---

[16] Confusion is often introduced into U.S. foreign policy by different U.S. agencies supporting different interests, sometimes leading to armed support for both sides in civil conflict with disastrous humanitarian results. A well-documented example is support for, and opposition to, Noriega in Panama.

[17] The Arab spring seems (Dec. 2012) to be marking a transition in status of some Arab nations from the second category to the first.

[18] As I write, my daily lesson on corporate behaviour is a review of a book on ExxonMobil detailing both the atrocities assisted by that corporation and its CEO's contempt for American labour: *Private Empire: ExxonMobil and American Power* by Steve Coll.

[19] As long ago as 1919 Edith Wharton wrote: 'How much longer are we going to think it necessary to be "American" before (or in contradistinc-

If corruptions of individual countries were catalogued by the commodities that inspired them, 'oil' would come top of the list. The tone of Western intervention was set by the deposition of the popularly-elected government of Mossadegh in Iran, who was ousted by the CIA and MI5 in 1953 after he moved to nationalize the oil industry.[20] The Shah, who by then had become more or less a 'constitutional monarch', was re-installed with totalitarian power, complete with weaponry, finance and torture equipment supplied by the West. The degradation of a country put through twenty-five years of such rule has been called somewhat euphemistically 'a setback in its political development'.[21] The Shah was later deposed in a populist revolution. The revolution installed a theocratic government which set itself to murder and make war on the grandest scale it could manage, in true revolutionary style. Subsequent 'oil wars' have been episodes 2, 3 and 4, etcetera, of this dirty opera.

A third characteristic of electoral representation highlighted in the 'export model' is the destruction of economic independence and of self-organized civil society at both local and national levels. The economist Peter Baer noted that it was the misfortune of many emerging African countries to adopt Western representative government just at the time when the Western model was evolving into one of all-pervasive state control. The prize handed to newly elected governments was administrative and economic monopoly by the state.

Despotism and kleptocracy do not inhere in the nature of African cultures; but they are now rife in what was once British co-

---

tion to) being cultivated, being enlightened, being humane, & having the same intellectual discipline as other civilized countries? It is really too easy a disguise for our shortcomings to dress them up as a form of patriotism!' Letter, July 19, 1919. *The Letters of Edith Wharton* (1988) p 424.

[20]   Stephen Kinzer, *All The Shah's Men* (2008).

[21]   By Secretary of State Madeleine K. Albright: Remarks before the American-Iranian Council (March 17, 2000). Presumably the remark was supposed to be in the way of an apology — or at least an acknowledgement of past injury.

lonial Africa… Many traditional African societies had leaders who acted capriciously, but they often governed rather lightly and with the consent of their subjects. It was the British policy of the closing years of colonialism that contributed greatly to the creation of a new political climate in which despotism was likely to emerge and corruption bound to flourish.[22]

Administration by the state destroys civil society: government professionals move in, displacing the activities of what are now called 'voluntary workers'. (Ironically, a return to civil society is now being mooted in the U.K.: governments have borrowed so much that their credit rating is no longer good, and they must live in terror of looming bankruptcy.)

In traditional societies 'voluntary workers' are not so much occasional do-gooders, as normal people exercising rights and fulfilling duties as active members of a community. These rights and duties are protected by tradition and in law. People's representatives, however, give themselves the power to change all that. Under the guise of 'democracy' officials are endowed with more-or-less arbitrary power and people obey them. As Tocqueville put it (talking of Europe and America): 'The same men who, from time to time, overturn a throne and trample kings, bow more and more, without resistance, to the slightest whim of a clerk.'[23]

In countries with traditional local and tribal power structures, centralization can lead to much worse outcomes than obsequiousness to clerks; it has led to exploitations, misappropriations, and the barbarities of ethnic murder mentioned above.

The most pervasive change that multi-party electoral representation brings to the life of a nation, however, is a change in the nature of politics itself. The elected assembly becomes not a forum for making impartial law but an arena in which interest groups compete for the distribution of money and

---

[22] 'Black Africa: the Living Legacy of Dying Colonialism' in *Reality and Rhetoric* (1984), pp 90-105; see also, 'Broadcasting the Liberal Death Wish' in *Equality, The Third World and Economic Delusion* (1981).

[23] *Democracy in America* Volume 2, Book 4, Chapter 5.

favours. After a while, it seems, this becomes what people think politics 'is' — negotiating, competing, conspiring for what you get from the state.[24] It is entirely forgotten that, one way or another, the state has taken a great deal more money off everyone before supplying some back.

The delirious joy felt by people emerging from tyranny into electoral representation is always widely reported in the media. If, later, there is a sense of disappointment among the 'newly democratised' it is not such big news. In *The Economist* of November 4th 2009, an article outlined the fact that, twenty years after the fall of most communist countries, only a half of citizens were happy with their transition to Western-style 'freedom and democracy'. A simple reason was given in the article: 'The belief that changes have benefited business and political elites far more than ordinary people is widespread.'

Since then, this 'belief' — perhaps 'noticing the obvious' would be a more accurate way of putting it — has spread throughout the so-called 'democratic world'. It seems that 'new democracies' cotton on quicker to just how undemocratic electoral representation turns out to be.

Movements such as Occupy spring up as intended forums for serious debate about the phenomenon. Mass corporate media have been mostly hostile, even scornful, to these movements. Serious debate of serious topics in these same media is thin-to-non-existent. Dissatisfaction is reported, however, when civil disobedience crosses legal boundaries. A Spanish student is quoted in the *New York Times* (September 27 2011) as saying "We are the first generation to say that voting is worthless."[25]

It is a sad outcome of 'representative democracy' that voting should have come to seem worthless. Voting is not worthless in itself, of course: it has come to seem so because the choice of who we can vote for has been captured by

---

[24]   Again, Bastiat's remark: 'The state is the great fictitious entity by which everyone seeks to live at the expense of everyone else.' *L'État*, 1848.

[25]   *New York Times* article about the 'Occupy' movement (September 27, 2011).

powerful interests. The popular expression of this seizure of authority by powers which should be under its control is: 'whoever you vote for, the government gets in'.[26]

---

26 This should surely be an old chestnut by now, part of common knowledge. For instance, an observation from 1878: 'Where the extent of the electoral district obliges constituents to vote for candidates who are unknown to them, the election is not free. It is managed by wire-pullers, and by party machinery, beyond the control of the electors.' Lord Acton, *The History of Freedom and Other Essays*, ed. John Neville Figgis and Reginald Vere Laurence (1907) available online at Liberty Fund.

Chapter Six

The Oligarchy Today: Corporations and Governments

Writers on politics have often remarked (somewhat wearily) that if only the powerful would behave themselves, almost any form of government would do.[1] But people motivated by a desire for power are not generally noted for their goodness. They tend to be unscrupulous and manipulative at the better end of the spectrum and murderously wicked at the worse. Personal ambition is a devious and duplicitous master: 'I am for the public good' it says, and the ambitious person is first to believe it.

The art of nation-making, as of law-making and of institution-building generally, is the art of containing power and ambition so that they act for, rather than against, the common good. The French philosopher Montesquieu put it baldly: 'It's a happy situation if, when we want to act badly, we find it's not in our interest to do so.'[2] In other words most of us are pleased to live in a society which restrains not only the wickedness of others, but also our own.

---

[1] The classic expression in English is by the poet Alexander Pope: 'For forms of government let fools contest / Whatever's best administered is best.'

[2] *De l'Esprit des Lois* XXI, 16 [20]. Albert Hirschbaum wrote a whole book (*The Passions and the Interests*) based on this sentence.

In all human societies there are individuals who have more power and influence than others, so an element of elitism, or oligarchy, is inevitable. The questions explored in this chapter are: What kind of oligarchy has electoral representation given us? Do our institutions and our elites serve our best interests? Is wickedness restrained or encouraged by our laws, our habits of government and our institutions? It's worth remembering that Darwin considered morality, along with intelligence, to be our most important asset for human survival.[3]

The oligarchy in the West today is obviously not a simple group of individuals like, say, the 'Thirty Tyrants' who ruled Athens for a year (404-3 BC), murdering people and making up laws at will. There are plenty such oligarchies in the world today and many of them are supported by Western interests, but power in the West itself is more widely dispersed. It is located in what is popularly called 'the system' (or just 'they'). 'The system' is an interconnected web of corporate bodies: among them governments, bureaucracies, business corporations (including the media), international treaty organizations (trade, military, policing, judicial and diplomatic), culture and policy foundations, military and labour organisations. These powers have (and need) a longer life-span than elected governments: for better and worse, they restrict the room for manoeuvre of elected officials. These are the powers that move our world. The job of political representatives, in practical reality, is to mediate between these powers and the voters.

Direct monitoring and control of these powers by voters *en masse* is unrealistic: no one has enough time and attention for it. But unless ordinary people, endowed with knowledge of what is going on, have an active influence in defining the limits and determining the operations of these powers, there is no meaningful democracy. It will be suggested in the last chapter of this book that some of these monitoring activities

---

3   *Descent of Man* Chapters 3, 4, 5. Like law, morality is continually changing in response to changing conditions; but unlike law, it cannot be reduced to a set of precepts.

might be better done in by political 'juries' than by elected representatives.

The huge expansion and proliferation of corporate powers accompanied a profound change in the world: a shift from human labour to machines as the source of what we consume. The consequences of this are immense: not only our hugely increased prosperity, but also the enforced idleness of large numbers of people, the ascendency of new talents (management, product design, salesmanship, financial speculation, technology etc.), the invention of more and more wasteful and destructive things to do, more individuals in the marketplace for power and celebrity, our Antaeus-like separation from Nature, the destructive potential of war, ever-increasing demands on the environment, and so on.[4]

The machines which produce our affluence today were made possible by new understandings of the natural world. In 1849, Mazzini (Italian nationalist and enthusiast of 'modernity') expressed great excitement at these developments. 'Collective man is omnipotent on the earth he treads!' he wrote. 'The age of individuality is over: we reformers must initiate the epoch of association!'[5] The dream of Mazzini and other believers was that humanity, united in purpose and a glorious common destiny, would move towards a shared enjoyment of the fruits of the earth: a community of liberty, equality and fraternity for all of humankind.

The dream foundered somewhat on the realities of collective enterprise. Collective enterprises need leaders. Leaders need power; they also need followers prepared to obey, even to guess what their leaders want before they ask. Moreover, collective enterprises are held together by a sense of common purpose and identity which excludes and competes with others. The culture of a collective enterprise—people

---

[4] Antaeus was a character in Greek myth who lost his strength when his feet were not on the ground. Hercules defeated him by holding him in the air.

[5] From *Watchword for the Roman Republic* (1849): quoted by Lewis Namier in 'Nationality and Liberty', reprinted in *Avenues of History* (1952) pp. 28ff.

brought together in a common purpose—could not be more different to that of a community—people living together in civility, out of common need. A collective enterprise (for instance an army) gives to an individual a sense of empowerment, but a loss of freedom; civil society means living within certain rules of conduct designed to restrict power and to enable freedom.[6]

Two of the great twentieth-century political attempts to organize 'collective man'—communism and fascism/Nazism—are remembered not for their equitable distribution of the new prosperity but for their 'murdering of millions on the cheap'.[7] Each of these ideologies thought they could combine political, judicial, cultural and commercial powers into a single state structure united by one shared ideology. The state itself became a collective enterprise, and in each case it took on the personality of a delinquent psychopath, hating now this, now that category of enemies (often imagined) and exercising lethal violence against them. Nothing in history could have prepared humanity for the huge and systematic slaughters perpetrated by these states. Leaders with previously unheard-of powers commanded vast administrations reaching into every nook and cranny of the nation. Their history is another testament (as if one was needed!) to the power, latent in corporate identity, of mustering human activity into mass immorality and crime.

The third way of managing industrial production and wealth—'market capitalism'—separates (in theory) corporate powers into 'government' and 'free enterprise'.[8] These

---

6   Michael Oakeshott has written extensively on this theme. His essay 'The Rule of Law' (in *On History*, 1983) is a summary.

7   The poet Osip Mandelstam's phrase. It is often forgotten that fascism and communism were forms of government by electoral representation, differing from what we are familiar with today in that they were one-party rather than multi-party states.

8   The word 'capitalism', now overloaded with emotional baggage, had a simple meaning long before Marx. 'Capital' is accumulated money hoping to make more money. 'Capitalism' is the doctrine which defends the use of privately-owned capital against those who would outlaw it. Capitalism becomes 'corporate' when individuals pool their money into larger enterprises with their own, separate legal identities.

two powers are not, however, so separate: dependent upon a common source of finance (see Chapter 4), they are sometimes cooperative, sometimes rivalrous. They may squabble like siblings over who gets the lion's share, but they are joined in being reliant on their power to command the labour and assets of others.

Not all corporations pursue money or power. A corporation is essentially just a number of people who come together in a common purpose. That purpose may be to play football, look after the local graveyard, or just have a good time. These purposes are self-limiting: if you are looking after the local graveyard, you only want to make it bigger when there are more people to bury.

The pursuit of money and power, however, has no natural limiting factor: the appetite for money and power is insatiable.[9] A corporation set up for the sole purpose of gaining more power or money is unlikely to practice self-restraint.[10]

An interesting writer on the nature of corporate association is Frederick William Maitland (1850-1906, sometimes called 'the greatest legal historian of all time').[11] He observed that it is human nature to collect in groups for a common purpose and that whenever an association is formed a sort of 'extra person' comes into being.[12]

---

[9] Burckhardt: 'Now power is in itself evil, no matter who wields it. It is not constant or dependable, but a lust and therefore insatiable. Unhappy in itself, it is bound to make others unhappy too.' From *Weltgeschichtliche Betrachtungen*.

[10] Governments often represent themselves as 'cutting back' but at the end of the process it is normally apparent that they have not 'cut back' their own power. Occasionally a power is genuinely dispensed with when it has proved too troublesome: for instance, running 'nationalised' businesses.

[11] In essays and talks: 'Trust and Corporation', 'The Corporation Sole', 'The Crown as Corporation', 'The Survival of Ancient Communities', 'The Unincorporated Body', 'Moral Personality and Legal Personality', 'The Body Politic' and his Introduction to Gierke's *Political Theories of the Middle Ages*. Many of these are available online.

[12] 'If n men unite themselves in an organised body, jurisprudence, unless it wishes to pulverise the group, must see $n+1$ persons.' Maitland, *Moral Personality And Legal Personality* (1903).

Take the example of a village football club. The club may carry on even if all the original members have left. It may own land and buildings. It will develop traditional ways of doing things, perhaps even a constitution. Villagers come and go, live and die, the football club lives on. It may exist happily for many years and never tangle with the law. But if, for instance, it has a dispute over a boundary with a neighbouring farmer it may need to sue, or be sued. If the conflict comes to law, the club must either be given a legal persona or reduced to the individuals who compose it: 'pulverised', as Maitland put it.

Curiously, Maitland praised the ability of corporate bodies to temporarily flout the law, thereby providing an area of 'social experimentation' where practices may be tried out and over time found to be either good or bad.

As an example, Maitland gave the way married women in England came to own property independently of their husbands.[13] First, the device of the 'trust' enabled rich women to benefit from property held on their behalf. Then, recognizing the unfairness of 'one law for the rich and another for the poor', parliament made it lawful for any married woman to own property.

The business corporation began in a similar manner. For many years, corporate property was held 'in trust' for investors. Only after many centuries was the law changed so that virtually anyone could form a separate corporate identity for purposes of doing business.[14]

Before that, corporations had to be licensed individually by the state.[15] Because they have their own separate and independent structures, only partly accountable to law and public scrutiny, even charitable corporations were regarded

---

[13]   The essay 'Trust and Corporation' (published 1911), available online at Liberty Fund.

[14]   A good overview is Cooke, *Corporation, Trust and Company* (1950).

[15]   Since the early sixteenth century, monarchs had licensed 'joint-stock' companies to trade and/or colonize in far-off countries: India, Russia, the Americas, the Far East and the West Indies. Encouraged by promised shares in the profits and the fact that the companies would be operating far away, monarchs allowed these enterprises corporate status.

as a potential threat to the health of the state. Hobbes (1588-1679) expressed this view when he declared that corporations in the State were 'as worms in the entrails of a natural man'.[16]

For more than two centuries after Hobbes, a battle raged over 'freedom of incorporation' — over whether a group of investors should be free to declare itself a commercial corporation and trade under a separate legal identity. The battle took place in England, Germany, France, Holland and the United States, and it was finally won by corporatists in those countries during the 1890's. Other countries followed suit.

Maitland, observing the activities of business corporations a few years after the law had fully acknowledged their existence, wrote: 'I rather think they must be damned'.[17] Of course they were not 'damned'; they were already far too powerful for that and too many people had vested interests in their existence.

For the next hundred years or so, Maitland's damnation was forgotten and the victory of the corporation (or company) was generally heralded as a victory for humanity. 'The company is Britain's most influential invention' declares a book published in 2003: 'this simple but brilliant idea has been one of the great catalysts of world history, acting as an engine for gathering in and pumping out money, goods, people and culture to every corner of the globe.'[18]

However, as the downsides of corporate business activity become more evident, the reasons why Maitland (and many of his contemporaries) thought the corporation should be damned are once again interesting. Historians have begun to explore the social context in which the battle for 'freedom of

---

[16] *Leviathan* II, 29.
[17] Letter to Henry Jackson, 18 Feb 1900. *Letters* (1965) pp. 212-3. In the same letter he said he intended to write a 'great treatise — *De Damnabilitate Universitatis* [On the Damnability of the Corporation].' He died six years later without publishing such a piece, his life cut short by illness.
[18] From the back cover of Micklethwait and Woolrich, *The Company: A Short History of a Revolutionary Idea* (2003).

incorporation' was won.[19] They have found that the corporation evolved not as a more efficient way of doing business, nor even from the wishes of businessmen, but in response to the needs and desires of a specific group—investors—who wanted to profit from commerce without any involvement in its day-to-day running, or any liability for debt and damage beyond their stake in the company.

Bank credit (see Chapter 4) vastly multiplied the amount of money available to these men for investment.[20]

The corporate form held several attractions for investors. It had a separate legal identity, which meant that individual shareholders were not liable for its debts.[21] It could sue and be sued in its own name, without involving each and every individual owner. It was in theory immortal, not vulnerable to disintegration or taxation on the deaths of its owners. It demanded no daily input of effort from investors. If it used rampant bad behaviour to increase profits, investors would remain blissfully unaware. Shares could be bought and sold in an open market. Certain key elements of the business— the composition of the board of directors, for instance— could be controlled by shareholders' votes. Finally, buying and selling shares had the excitement of a horse-race; it transformed business ownership into a gambling venture.

Such were its attractions. The opposition to 'freedom of incorporation' was made up of almost everyone except investors and company promoters.[22] Merchants and busi-

---

[19] For instance, *Making the Market* by Paul Johnson (2010) and *Creating Capitalism* by James Taylor (2006).

[20] P.G.M. Dickson, *The financial revolution in England: a study in the development of public credit, 1688-1756* (1967). Credit-creation was a key factor in Britain's rise to global pre-eminence during the 18th and 19th centuries.

[21] Limited liability and incorporation were, from the start, inseparable. 'As these corporations were legal entities quite distinct from their members, it followed that at common law the members were not liable for the debts of the corporation, and, indeed, the Crown had no power to incorporate persons so as to make them liable for the debts of the corporation.' John Charlesworth, *The Principles of Company Law* (1932), p. 1.

[22] Books about this: B.C. Hunt, *The Development of the Business Corporation in England*, 1800-1867 (1936); Micklethwait & Wooldridge *The Company* (2003).

nessmen resented the idea of privileged competition. The economist Adam Smith stressed their inefficiency, their wastefulness and the opportunities they offered for dishonest behaviour.[23] Jurists stressed their imperviousness to both law and moral opprobrium: 'they have neither bodies to imprison, nor souls to save or damn'.[24] Many (including Adam Smith) objected to their 'limited liability': if the corporation took on large debts and went bankrupt, the owners could avoid digging in their pockets to pay creditors. Why should speculators be given the privilege of reneging on business debts?[25]

The battle raged on and off throughout the 18th and 19th centuries and the 'moneyed interest' — would-be investors and company promoters — eventually won. Limited liability became freely available in English law during the 1850's; the corporation was recognized as a legal entity both in England and in America during the 1890's.[26]

A practical problem faced investors: how could they ensure that profits went to them, rather than to workers in the company? How could they restrain managers and workers from taking bites out of the business, as hyenas take bites from a running cow?[27] The solution they found was to ready

---

[23] *Wealth of Nations* Liberty Fund edition (available online) p. 741.

[24] This sentence was much-quoted by Victorian commentators: for instance, by Lord Acton in correspondence with Mary Gladstone (May 7 1881). Its origin is uncertain.

[25] 'Nothing can be so unjust as for a few persons abounding in wealth, to offer a portion of their excess for the formation of a company, to play with that excess — to lend the importance of their whole name and credit to the society, and then should the funds prove insufficient to answer all demands, to retire into the security of their unhazarded fortune, and leave the bait to be devoured by the poor deceived fish.' Leading article, *The Times* May 25, 1824, quoted Hunt p. 29. Adam Smith also objected to limited liability: *Wealth of Nations* (Liberty Fund, available online) p. 757.

[26] Limited liability was already a legal and practical reality for authorised 'joint-stock' companies; see B.C. Hunt *The Development of the Business Corporation in England, 1800-1867* (1936) pp. 116-144. The real argument was about extending the privilege to all and sundry.

[27] It is perhaps an irony that the much-trumpeted British invention of the business corporation coincided with the beginning of the decline of Brit-

to hand: the way they picked it up and used it is a preview of much else in the corporate book of tricks. They took a clause common to all corporate charters, put there to restrain corporate activity, and turned it to their advantage.

Corporations, to be recognized in law, had to state their purpose and stick to it: a corporation devoted to caring for the elderly of Bradford, for instance, could not depart from its 'object in law' and launch an invasion of France. Investors put as their 'object in law' the purpose of making as much money as possible for themselves. By this device, the full force of law was put behind investors: they would be the ones to profit, not just from the labour of workers and managers, but also from advances in technology, communications and systems management.[28] The surplus fruits of all corporate labour would from thenceforth all be theirs. Any employee straying from the purpose of 'maximising shareholder value' would be breaking the law. This system is what U.S. Supreme Court Justice Brandeis (1933) referred to as a new feudalism, a 'Frankenstein monster' and 'the negation of industrial democracy'.[29]

Many writers have pointed out that the obligation to 'maximise shareholder value' has now been to a large extent frustrated by senior managers and providers of 'financial services', who manage to divert most of the profit for themselves.[30] The struggle to profit from the work of others, in-

---

ish industry (1890's). The connection has not, so far as I know, been investigated, though it might seem obvious that the cantankerous independent-mindedness often noticed in British culture does not sit easily with 'corporate serfdom'. 'Britain is a world by itself and we will nothing pay for wearing our own noses,' says the obstreperous Cloten in Shakespeare's *Cymbeline*.

[28] This is presumably one of the things that people object to in 'capitalism': the legal privileging of capitalistic business structures.

[29] Justice Brandeis (in dissent), Liggett Co. v Lee, 1933. Quoted in *The Future of Democratic Capitalism* (1950), p.52.

[30] Berle & Means (1932); Galbraith (1967); F. Mount (2012). For a defence of corporate structure and behaviour see, for instance, Ian B. Lee, 'Is There a Cure for Corporate "Psychopathy"?' in *American Business Law Journal* 42, 2005, pp. 65 – 90.)

cluding people long dead (inventors, scientists, ancestors etc.), and from the capacity of machines, is an inequitable one, made even more inequitable by the capacity of banks and governments to create money.

Corporations resemble humans in that they need a home: a place of incorporation. Since the 1890's, states and countries have competed by lowering taxes and standards of regulation, and encouraging their judiciaries to be friendly to corporate interests, in order to attract revenue which comes from hosting corporations. The U.S. State of Delaware currently hosts the most corporations—many thousands are often 'domiciled' in one room—and provides the most congenial environment for corporate 'freedoms'. Competition between States to accommodate corporate misbehaviour is known as 'a race to the bottom'.

Concerning the various privileges available to business corporations, it has been suggested that if a privilege is available to anyone upon request it becomes 'democratic' and loses its negative character.[31] The privilege of a business corporation, however, is attached to a way of doing things. The corporation is privileged as a way of doing business: it became the dominant form not because it is more efficient, or for any other virtue, but simply because privilege gives it advantage over other forms.[32]

The dominance of the business corporation has profoundly altered the human and natural world in all of its aspects: occupational, cultural, political, natural, moral, intellectual, environmental. Its 'object in law' deprives it of the

---

[31] For instance, Bishop C. Hunt ends his book referred to above with this celebration of corporate privilege: 'After more than a century of struggle against deeply rooted prejudice and widespread misconception, freedom of incorporation was accomplished fact. The joint-stock company, and the indispensable incident of limited liability, both at first prohibited except under special and rare Parliamentary discretion or favour and later a carefully guarded bureaucratic concession, were privileges to be recognised as of common right.' — Bishop C. Hunt, *The Development of the Business Corporation in England, 1800-1867* (1936).

[32] There have traditionally been certain exceptions: cooperatives, partnerships, single proprietorships, but most of these have now also adopted corporate status and limited liability.

moral dimension which makes humanity able to use its clev-
erness with intelligence—that is, with regard to its future. A
corporation is a hierarchy: directors, management, workers
all governed by an obligation to produce profit.[33] A corporation is legally debarred from taking moral considerations
into account unless doing so can be shown to increase
'shareholder value'.[34]

Recent attempts to mitigate this by tinkering with the 'object in law' requirement have proved largely ineffectual.
Pressure from environmental and social welfare groups has
pushed governments to impose other duties on corporations
besides 'maximising shareholder value'. In Britain, for instance, Section 172 of the Companies Act 2006 obliges directors to (among other things) 'have regard to the impact of
the company's operations on the community and the environment', but only in the context of promoting 'the success
of the company for the benefit of its members as a whole'
('members' means owners). In practice, when these obligations conflict with each other, courts are reluctant to adjudi-
cate. Bill Davies sums up the situation:

> Two factors militate strongly against the use of Section 172 as a
> litigation weapon. Firstly, Section 172 is highly subjective. This
> means that the courts will remain unwilling to interfere in mat-
> ters of commercial judgment providing that the directors have
> acted in good faith. Bad faith is very difficult to prove.
>
> Secondly, the classes of litigants are effectively limited to the
> company itself (to whom the duty is owed) and shareholders
> pursuing a derivative action. Historically, derivative actions
> were rarely successful and even under the new statutory deriva-
> tive action there are many procedural obstacles to bringing a

---

[33] This point is emphasised also by defenders of the business corporation:
see, for instance, Elaine Sternberg, *Just Business* (1994) p. 35. An extreme
example of the routinization of immorality, all the more interesting for
its element of psychological autobiography, is narrated in *Confessions of
an Economic Hitman* by John Perkins (2004).

[34] The classic case is Dodge v. Ford Motor Company (1919).

claim. The various stakeholders referred to in Section 172 do not have *locus standi* to bring an action.[35]

The ambiguity does, however, allow some freedom to directors, and the culture within corporations is becoming more variable. Some corporations are more conscientious, others less so, depending upon individual directors, shareholder demands, the nature of the product and possibly even consumer response to corporate good behaviour.

Corporations can, of course, be fined; but they cannot realistically be punished (you can't put a whole corporation in prison). A multitude of extra legislation and regulation has been introduced to restrain corporate bribery, plunder, corruption, theft, oppression, pollution, injury, monopoly, exploitation etcetera. The effectiveness of this huge volume of regulations (the U.K. 2006 Companies Act alone runs to 700 pages) is compromised by two factors. First, companies influence the regulatory bodies so that laws and regulations are made in their favour (so-called 'regulatory capture').[36] Second, the proliferation of regulations favours larger corporations which can afford special departments to cope with them. Small independent competitors cannot afford the immense task of satisfying regulations designed for gigantic enterprises but which also apply to the smallest.[37]

The undying nature of the corporation means that once the founder is out of the way, the hierarchy will be dominated by individuals selected for adeptness at the corporate game: seeking opportunity, intuitively understanding what is required of them, undermining rivals, putting morality to one side, evading law when necessary and corrupting it

---

[35] Bill Davies, 'More Than the Bottom Line' in *New Law Journal*, 158, Issue 7331, 2008.

[36] Stigler, 'The Theory of Economic Regulation' in *Bell Journal of Economics and Management* 2, 1971. So-called 'deep capture' refers to corporations using their power to influence academia, media and popular culture.

[37] Vandana Shiva (*Protect or Plunder*, 2001) has chronicled how company law and regulations drive out small competitors in India. *Prophets of Regulation* by Thomas McCraw chronicles the failure of regulation to achieve simple objectives (and the frequent achievement of the opposite of what was intended).

when possible. The selectivity of corporations, determining the kind of individuals who become influential in 'capitalist' societies, is a significant determining factor in our world. In every department of human life and activity, corporate structures replace civil structures and the world is remodelled as an affluence-producing enterprise.

As for workers, it pays to dispense with moral considerations in the workplace. A job is a job: wheat today, weapons tomorrow. Responsibility lies elsewhere.

As individuals, most humans are by nature preoccupied with moral considerations: how to live a good life, feel pride in work, do well by our fellow humans, etcetera. Amassed in groups and under a leader, however, people shed those considerations and accept codes of behaviour—such as loyalty to the group—which drive them out. Of course, the world of business has always had its scoundrels, but with the dominance of corporations we might say that moral dereliction has become global and obligatory.

The largest business corporations are now larger in economic terms than most nations. They depend upon national governments to take care of their 'externalities': discarded workers, social problems, pollution. Both powers gain from this arrangement: corporations from enhanced profits, governments from extensions of their powers; but society loses for familiar reasons—expanding debt, diminishing competitiveness of the labour force, loss of freedom, and perhaps most of all, a miserable loss of pride in human life and civilization. The combined rule of these superpowers has been called variously 'soft totalitarianism'[38], 'the new feudalism'[39], 'liberal fascism'[40], 'friendly fascism'[41] 'neo-liberalism'[42] and 'volunteered slavery'[43].

---

[38] Origin unknown, but perhaps Roland Huntford, *The New Totalitarians* (1972).

[39] Supreme Court Justice Brandeis (in dissent), *Liggett Co. v Lee*, 1933. Quoted in *The Future of Democratic Capitalism* (1950), p. 52.

[40] Title of a book by Jonah Goldberg (2007).

[41] Title of a book by Bertram Gross (1980).

[42] N. Chomsky, *Profit over People: Neoliberalism and Global Order* (1998).

[43] Title of a musical work by Rahsaan Roland Kirk, 1968.

There is an analogy to the business corporation in myth: the Golem of Prague. The Golem was a monster of clay created by the Rabbi to do his housework and protect him from anti-Semites. The clay monster was given life by a magic inscription written on a piece of paper—a certificate of incorporation, you might say. But the Golem developed a life and will of its own and became unmanageable, crashing around and causing all kinds of murder and mayhem. The Rabbi eventually removed the certificate of incorporation and the monster became clay again.

We are told it is impossible to follow the example of the Rabbi of Prague and de-authorise the corporation. If that is the case, I would say our civilization is in peril. Of all the achievements of the corporation, the most perilous is to have shifted our understanding of the word 'freedom' from 'the freedom to do what one believes is right' to 'the freedom to consume anything and everything, right to the end of the world.'

Evidently, not all corporations are doomed to act immorally. As noted above, corporate bodies exist for many purposes: most are defined within clear and respectable limits, not to feed the potentially insatiable appetites of money and power. A corporation's purpose is clearly expressed in its charter. It is licensed on the understanding that neither its purpose, nor the way it pursues it, are destructive of the public interest.

A corporate body (trade union) may, for instance, be set up to protect the interests of a certain group of workers. The power of such a body lies not just in its ability to muster the combined force of its members, but also in public authorization of its existence which is conditional (we might say) on its good behaviour vis-à-vis the rest of us. When it oversteps the line, it is (eventually, and by general agreement) restrained. The same condition (in theory) exists for any corporate body, set up for any purpose whatsoever.

This condition should also apply to government. There has always been a corporate element to government, which must operate as a legal entity beyond, and partially independent of, the people who compose it. Monarchs are corporations: as law developed in the Middle Ages, the monarchy, or crown, became the legal entity, not the person in temporary occupation of it.[44] Under republican government, a legal designation such as 'The State', 'The People' or 'The United States' signifies 'the (corporate) body that rules'.

Government is a unique kind of corporate entity in that membership is obligatory. Most corporate associations are optional: we can choose whether or not to belong to them. But governments are different. We have to live somewhere, and whether we like it or not we must live under the government of that somewhere.

Because of this, Western political thinkers interested in freedom have always wanted to limit the power of the state. Freedom means choosing one's own purpose in life. The state should not impose a common purpose on its citizens: on the contrary, it should enable the freedom of citizens to pursue their own purposes, within a rule of law.[45]

Electoral representation, however, has changed what people expect from government. When parties compete for election they undertake to transform our lives for the better. As a result they absorb us all in a purpose: the creation of an affluent, fair society, full of good and prosperous citizens.[46] If only this was what they delivered, how happy we would be! The trouble is, in the words of Michael Oakeshott, 'The outcome of trying to make the state a paradise has always been to turn it into a hell.'[47] By taking from some, giving to others, regulating lives, taking on duties that bind families and communities together, governments create atomized, dependent and anonymous masses of citizens for whom (according to one public celebrity) 'the worm-hole of celebrity is their only escape'.

---

44   See Maitland's essay 'The Crown as Corporation' (1901).
45   For an elaboration of this see Michael Oakeshott, *On Human Conduct* (1975), parts 2, 3; also 'Talking Politics' (*Rationalism in Politics*, 1991).
46   This has been much commented upon. See, for instance, books by John Gray: *Black Mass* (2008), *Straw Dogs* (2003) and *False Dawn* (2009).
47   Michael Oakeshott, *On Human Conduct* (1990) p. 319n.

The more governments fail in their attempts to create a perfect society, the more they promise to do better next time.[48] They take more power, more money: government becomes the biggest employer. Political parties come and go, but the power of the state keeps growing until now—as previously mentioned—many absorb close to 50% of their nations' incomes.

The growing patronage of government means we all look to it for favours, if not for outright employment. A mentality of resentful dependence grows among citizens, a grudging servility to a power they neither admire nor know how to escape.[49]

Governments live off their citizens so (in the best sense of the word) they are inevitably parasitic. By taking over functions which used to be a matter for society, however, they become something more like a malignant tumour. It might be said we live in an oncocracy, were that not such an unlikely word.

In practice, the downward spiral of state control is limited. The state must eventually go bankrupt when it indebts its citizens to such an extent that it cannot borrow more.

John Locke, that quintessentially respectable philosopher, wrote that the people will put up with many abuses before they 'rouse themselves and endeavour to put the rule into such hands which may secure to them the ends for which government was at first erected'.[50] Unless we re-discover

---

[48] In his book *Visions of the Anointed* (1995) Thomas Sowell chronicles many of the projects of liberal utopianism from conception to outcome—from promised heavens to delivered hells.

[49] John Stuart Mill quoting Royer Collard (1862): 'when the satisfaction of every public want is a favour of the administration, the power of government is assured... We have not yet noticed the great moral and political mischief of training a people to be one vast tribe of place-hunters.' 'Centralisation' (1862); available on the Liberty Fund website.

[50] 'Great mistakes in the ruling part, many wrong and inconvenient laws, and all the slips of human frailty, will be born by the people without mutiny or murmur. But if a long train of abuses, prevarications and artifices, all tending the same way, make the design visible to the people, and they cannot but feel what they lie under, and see whither they are going; it is not to be wondered, that they should then rouze themselves, and

'the ends for which government was at first erected' we will hardly know what to 'rouse ourselves' for. Democracy and freedom are candles in our darkness. If we recover their meanings, we can begin to recover their practice.

The main political parties in most Western countries are descendents of the ideologies of left and right – of big state and big business. After expelling their extremists, these ideologies began to form a working consensus. Alternating in power, political parties give more now to the state, more now to business.

Propaganda for the powers of commerce and state is the background noise to everyday life: advertising, news, opinion-makers, party apologists, trash culture. How culture has been degraded is a subject for a different book: suffice it to say here, that the dream of power, which is subjection, is antagonistic to the dream of human culture, which is freedom.

The battle against corporate ownership and domination in the media was lost over half a century ago. In 1950 Morris L. Ernst lamented 'we have lost one thousand daily newspapers in the last two decades, and what is more important than the dailies, twenty-five hundred weeklies in the small towns of America have disappeared.'[51] He added: 'democracy is a "grass roots" process, and the level of democracy cannot rise above the level of diversity of opinion within the smallest hamlet.' Corporate ownership of the media is now close to 100% and American public opinion has suffered as a result.

The outcome of this battle lost was summed up by George Kennan:

---

endeavour to put the rule into such hands which may secure to them the ends for which government was at first erected; and without which, ancient names, and specious forms, are so far from being better, that they are much worse, than the state of nature, or pure anarchy; the inconveniencies being all as great and as near, but the remedy farther off and more difficult.' *Second Treatise on Civil Government* (1693), Ch. 19.

51   Morris Ernst, 'The Preservation of Civil Liberties' in *The Future of Democratic Capitalism* (1950) p. 19.

I suspect that what purports to be public opinion in most countries that consider themselves to have popular government is often not really the consensus of the feelings of the mass of the people at all but rather the expression of the interests of special highly vocal minorities — politicians, commentators, and publicity-seekers of all sorts: people who live by their ability to draw attention to themselves and die, like fish out of water, if they are compelled to remain silent. These people take refuge in pat and chauvinistic slogans because they are incapable of understanding any others, because these slogans are safer from the standpoint of short term gain, because the truth is sometimes a poor competitor in the marketplace of ideas — complicated, unsatisfying, full of dilemmas, always vulnerable to misinterpretation and abuse. The counsels of impatience and hatred can always be supported by the crudest and cheapest symbols; for the counsels of moderation, the reasons are often intricate, rather than emotional, and difficult to explain. And so the chauvinists of all times and places go their appointed way: plucking the easy fruits, reaping the little triumphs of the day at the expense of someone else tomorrow, deluging in noise and filth anyone who gets in their way, dancing their reckless dance on the prospects for human progress, drawing the shadow of a great doubt over the validity of democratic institutions.[52]

More recently, the development of the internet spawned hopes that we might see a new generation of informed and thoughtful citizens. So far (2012) it uses are primarily pornography, entertainment and shopping; but these are early days. Availability of information and easy outreach of opinion make all kinds of things possible. The struggle to maintain freedom on the internet is perhaps the most important struggle taking place at this time.

In academic institutions, freedom of thought and expression is in retreat in many areas. Administrators of universities have become top-down representatives of government, rather than defenders of the independence of their institutions. Funding is sought from corporations as well as governments: 'market forces' is a euphemism for conformity to corporate demands.

---

[52] George Kennan, *American Diplomacy* (expanded edition, 2012) p 66.

'Political correctness' affects many academic disciplines. Like all tyrannical ideologies, it masquerades as concern for the underdog but supports the rise of a new overdog. While seeming to promote multiculturalism, it denies genetic variety among human beings and forbids analysis of what kinds of human are (temporarily) favoured by the peculiar conditions of human life today. This buries the urgent need of some peoples to enjoy protection from the ravages of Western imperialism. If we are all the same, the argument goes, we all deserve to 'enjoy' the benefits of Western ways of life.[53]

As for the natural world, its treatment by corporations and governments is chronicled in books and magazines available to anyone who cares to know.[54] They make painful reading, inducing a combined sense of complicity and helplessness which is hard to bear. One can know enough; one can know too much; one has, after all, to live.

Corporations put aside large budgets for 'lobbying'.[55] When the Congress of the United States is described as 'a forum for legalized bribery'[56] no one bothers to disagree — and no nation suspects its own representative assembly of anything much better.

The 'metamorphosis of liberalism into its opposite'[57] is a theme explored by many writers from Burckhardt through to Oakeshott, John Gray and Thomas Sowell. Promising to rectify unfairness, governments undertake all kinds of 'never-heard-of and outrageous tasks'.[58] S.E. Finer quotes the following text by the French anarchist Proudhon on the na-

---

53 'Enjoy' is in inverted commas because surveys suggest Westerners are generally, compared to the rest of humanity, somewhat miserable. See *The Spirit Level* (2010) by Richard Wilkinson and Kate Pickett.

54 For instance, *The Ecologist* magazine.

55 Lobbying involves attempts to block restrictive legislation, to gain government contracts, subsidies and other privileges; and also to claim for corporations those rights guaranteed in law to human persons.

56 *The New York Times*, Oct 31, 2011.

57 Oakeshott's phrase: *The Vocabulary of a Modern European State* (2008) p. 124.

58 Burckhardt's phrase, quoted in *Reflections on History* (1979) intro, p.22.

ture of intrusive government. The description is extreme and of its time (1871), but is nevertheless a familiar picture of how powerful, well-meaning government operates 'for our own good':

> To be governed is to be kept in sight, inspected, spied upon, directed, law-driven, numbered, enrolled, indoctrinated, preached at, controlled, estimated, valued, censured, commanded, by creatures who have neither the right, nor the wisdom, nor the virtue to do so.... To be governed is to be at every operation, at every transaction, noted, registered, enrolled, taxed, stamped, measured, numbered, assessed, licensed, authorized, admonished, forbidden, reformed, corrected, punished. It is, under the pretext of public utility, and in the name of the general interest, to be placed under contribution, trained, ransomed, exploited, monopolized, extorted, squeezed, mystified, robbed; then, at the slightest resistance, the first word of complaint, to be repressed, fined, despised, harassed, tracked, abused, clubbed, disarmed, choked, imprisoned, judged, condemned, shot, deported, sacrificed, sold, betrayed; and, to crown all, mocked, ridiculed, outraged, dishonored. That is government; that is its justice; that is its morality. And to think that there are democrats among us who pretend that there is good in government; socialists who support this ignominy in the name of Liberty, Equality, and Fraternity; proletarians who proclaim their candidacy for the Presidency of the Republic![59]

We should be able to do better than that in the name of 'freedom and democracy'!

---

[59] S.E. Finer, The History of Government (OUP 1997) p. 1610. From Proudhon's *General Idea of the Revolution in the Nineteenth Century* (1851) tr. J.B. Robinson.

Chapter Seven

Democracy and Good Government

'The fundamental change which Democracy long ago commenced, was not from this particular law to that, but from the despotism of one to the freedom of all.' — *Herbert Spencer*

The tyrant of Libya, Muammar Gaddafi, instituted a government which was in theory perfectly democratic.[1] It had, however, a simple addition: a hierarchy of informants, controlled from top down, who listened to what was being said and delivered up critics of the regime for imprisonment, torture and murder. So easy is it to corrupt the best of ideas into the worst of realities. If we decide to make our Western systems more democratic, it's worth remembering there are worse forms of government waiting in the wings, some of which may begin with a greater claim to being democratic.

And yet, without some elements of true and binding democracy we will remain what we are: citizens reduced by elites to dependency and debt, engulfed in a culture of relentless growth and consumerism which endangers all our futures, and yet helpless to effect any change.[2]

There is another factor to democracy: as citizens we can only be politically 'alive' by being involved. For many (but

---

[1] Gaddafi's *The Green Book Part One: The Solution of the Problem of Democracy* describes a structure of government where all rule originates in popular assemblies.

[2] As Chapter 4 makes clear, relentless consumption is necessary not because we all desire it, but to keep our inequitable system of money-creation from collapse.

not everyone) being politically alive is like being able to breathe. What kind of society do we want to create for ourselves? In truly democratic communities, political participation is not a profession but a right — and perhaps also a duty, in the way that jury service is a duty in many countries.

The problems addressed in this chapter will be: what mechanisms of democracy might contribute to good government, and how might they be implemented?

Preliminary Considerations

1. What is 'good government'?

There is some disagreement about what kind of government is good, so I start with a list of features which I assume most people want from government. Most people might agree, for instance, that good government:

> Creates fair, just and disinterested laws which are properly enforced.
>
> Maintains good relations as far as possible and deals justly with other states.
>
> Employs no violence against its own citizens beyond what is unavoidable for and within due process of law.
>
> Prevents the powerful from exploiting the vulnerable.
>
> Protects the ecological and human assets of the nation and restrains its citizens from destroying those of other nations.
>
> Allows no agencies of coercion other than its own.
>
> Secures the nation from invasion, economic despoliation, and other outside abuses.
>
> Avoids rather than seeks out war.
>
> By clear, open and good governance, inspires the loyalty and allegiance of its citizens.
>
> Protects the interests of future generations.
>
> Is open to, but careful of, initiatives for change.

2: The increasingly federal, or layered, nature of government today

Over the last hundred years or so, a proliferation of international powers exercising authority over nation states has changed the nature of political power and its relationship with ordinary people. This development shows no signs of stopping; and in an age of nuclear weaponry, transnational pollution, dependence upon fossil fuels and globalised finance most people would say we need more international law and authority, not less.

For several hundred years, the nation state was the standard political entity of the West. In these entities 'the state' was a single authority with the exclusive right to exercise force.[3] The tendency now, in a world ever more connected and more crowded, has been towards layered government, roughly a development of the old idea of 'federalism'. If you live in a district called Littleton you are ruled in certain matters (perhaps in how and when you put out your rubbish) by the authority constituted for Littleton; in other matters (perhaps on whether you are allowed to open up a supermarket) by the larger unit of Big County; in other matters, by the criminal code of the state as modified by the agreements of a federal union; in yet other matters—for instance, if you join in state-sponsored genocide—you might find yourself before a world court.

Your activities as a trader, meanwhile, will be governed in a separate, floating system of international commercial law which at present depends upon sovereignty of contract, national law (or lack of it) and a variety of trade agreements and treaties.

The rest of international law, meanwhile, struggles with questions such as: should it champion the rights of individuals against their local or national authorities? Should it merely govern the behaviour of states towards one another? To what extent can it resist being manipulated by great states—or being used by smaller states to persecute great

---

3   Max Weber carrying to its logical conclusion the State theorised by
     Hobbes as *Leviathan* and Bodin as 'sovereignty absolute and indivisible'.

ones? What is its relationship with international commercial law? International law at present has jurisdiction only by treaties between nations — and treaties can be disowned or ignored by national governments (especially powerful ones) when they see fit.

All these levels and divisions of government busy themselves with negotiating and re-negotiating the limits of their areas of authority, power and responsibility, always with the assumption that electoral representation supplies the consent of their 'peoples'. As popular consent withdraws (fewer people voting, less and less trust and respect for those in power, more and more awareness of corruptions and inequities; apathy, frustration and helplessness among nonpoliticians) the question naturally arises: how can real democracy find an institutional home for itself among these layers of power? How can the interests of ordinary people survive, let alone compete, among the interests of the powerful?

We are told that the important divisions in government are between executive, legislature and judiciary. What of the older division, between the interests of rich and poor?[4] Ignoring this division has made it easier for one class to seize the ascendant: the rich become richer; the poor become poorer; the middle (often unwittingly) find themselves serving the interests of the rich. Because the rich have power anyway by virtue of being rich, and the middle class have power in their relationship to the rich and their control of the workings of society, democracy must effectively mean (just as it did in Aristotle's time) including the poor in the structures of power.[5] When power is divided between executive,

---

[4]   Acton: 'By his idea that the powers of government ought to be divided according to their nature, and not according to the division of classes, which Montesquieu took up and developed with consummate talent, Locke is the originator of the long reign of English institutions in foreign lands.' — from 'The History of Freedom in Christianity' available at Liberty Fund and other places online.

[5]   There are continual efforts to re-define democracy as something other than 'rule by all', usually something more woolly: 'guaranteed civil rights', 'equality of opportunity', 'fair distribution' etc. The result is that

legislature and judiciary, there must be democratic elements in each of these powers; as also in the control and monitoring of the money supply.

The establishment of democracy is one thing, its preservation another. However much there may be of democracy at any one time, there will always be people and institutions trying, by fair means and foul, to suppress it and get more power for themselves. In other words, democracy, like freedom, needs continual defence and protection.[6]

3: Electoral representation, democracy and good government

The claim of electoral representation to be a form of democracy rests on three assertions: that ordinary people choose political agents to act on their behalf; that we all have access to our representatives; and that anyone can become a politician. The first two assertions are weakened by the power of political parties. Political parties select candidates and present them for election and candidates must be loyal to their party. Merely having access to such a representative is neither rule, nor power, nor authority, and therefore nothing to do with democracy. The last assertion, that anyone can become a politician, neglects the fact that not everyone wants to become a professional politician, nor would society function if they did. There can only be real democracy where power is not concentrated among paid professionals, but disseminated among non-politicians. As soon as a paid professional appears on the scene, self-government leaves by the back door.

The easiest way to limit the power of political parties is for representatives to vote in secret in the assembly. This

---

anyone can claim to be 'democratic' simply by adopting a suitable definition. The poor, meanwhile, stay powerless. For Aristotle, see *Politics*, Bk. 3, Ch. 8.

6   'It is by the combined efforts of the weak, made under compulsion, to resist the reign of force and constant wrong, that liberty has been preserved.' Acton, *Lectures in Modern History*, p. 289.

practice was recommended by Montesquieu[7] and it would mean that representatives could not be coerced to vote against their consciences.[8]

Indirect election has been suggested as a way of selecting better representatives. Meetings of citizens are held at local level, where numbers are small enough for voters to be familiar with the candidates.[9] Those elected locally represent the neighbourhood at the next level up.[10] This process can be repeated to supply representatives at any number of levels.[11] It is only effective if at the lowest level people know each other: that is, if the lowest assembly is at neighbourhood level.[12] At present, indirect election is used mostly to choose elites within elites: for political parties, and elected representatives, to choose among their number for higher office.[13]

It is interesting that in Switzerland, where there is a high level of democracy, political parties do not have strong central organisations. Significant debate about legislation takes place among the people, who have the final say (see later in

---

[7]   *De L'Esprit Des Lois*, Book 2, Chapter 2.

[8]   This conflicts with the idea of the 'mandate': that representatives should be seen to keep their promises to 'the people'. However, the idea of the mandate is unrealistic both in theory (circumstances are always changing) and in practice (the corrupting nature of power).

[9]   Arthur D. Robbins, in *Paradise Lost, Paradise Regained* (2012) draws attention to Thomas Jefferson's suggestion of ward meetings as the basis for true electoral democracy (p. 419). Hannah Arendt discusses Jefferson's proposals at length in *On Revolution* (1963).

[10] Some of the problems that present themselves: at what point do representatives become recompensed or paid professionals? Are they representatives or delegates, i.e. can they change their minds as a result of higher-level deliberation or is this a betrayal of their neighbourhood group? How obligatory is it for people to attend, or to represent? How are meetings organised so that busy people can attend? How much time is involved? Are representative duties organised so that busy people may fulfil them?

[11] 'If the intermediate body consisted of one in ten of the whole constituency, the contact would be preserved, the people would be really represented.' Acton in *Democracy in Europe* (available online at Liberty Fund).

[12] 'Sociocracy' is a practical development of this kind of indirect election. A summarising article of the process, *Sociocracy* by Kees Boeke, is available fairly widely on the internet.

[13] Wikipedia article *Indirect Election* as of 19/09/2012.

this chapter); politics in the elected assemblies is less relevant and somewhat lifeless.[14]

Local assemblies create a sense of community. When representatives manage everything from above, the political involvement of the average citizen is reduced to the solitary act of voting. Communities do not arise by magic, but out of necessity. Self-government leads to active participation and to community. This is presumably what Rousseau had in mind when he wrote that 'the moment a people allows itself to be represented, it is no long free: it no longer exists.'[15]

4: Self-government, democracy and good government

'Self-government' and 'democracy' may seem to be identical in meaning. Surely, if the people are governing themselves, that is democracy? If, however, there is self-government on a local level, but overall power and authority are at a higher level (perhaps with a monarch or emperor) then it is only a limited form of democracy.

For instance, in the ancient world certain Greek city states were embedded in the Persian empire. They were allowed to rule themselves, but they had to pay taxes to the Persian king. If they caused trouble, the forces of the empire would come down terribly upon them. It has been said that some of these were the happiest places on earth: Greek citizens could indulge their passion and genius for self-government, but were unable to exercise their passion and genius for war.[16]

Another interesting example is 'self-government at the king's command'.[17] In England in the late Middle Ages, monarchs encouraged local self-government so that they could get on with doing what they really wanted — which

---

14   Jonathan Steinberg, *Why Switzerland* (1996), pp 112-3.

15   *The Social Contract*, tr. G.D.H. Cole. Book III, Chapter 15.

16   I believe that was S.E. Finer's opinion; I cannot locate the reference.

17   This is the title of an influential book by A.B.Whyte (1933). Other writers on (local) self-government in England: Sidney and Beatrice Webb (9 volumes), Rudolf Gneist, Josef Redllich, Bryan Keith-Lucas, Peter Laslett, Patrick Collinson, Paul Vinogradoff.

was usually to make war.[18] As a result, a great variety of local administrations flourished over many centuries: some democratic, some oligarchic, some tyrannical, all enclosed in a system of interlocking rights and duties.[19]

All these local autonomies were eventually swept away in reforms during the nineteenth century and replaced by top-down administration.[20] These top-down reforms were applauded by liberals at home but were greatly criticized by liberals abroad, who were accustomed to seeing England as a bastion of constitutional freedom.[21] The German jurist Rudolf Gneist, for instance, remarked sadly that removing the rights and duties of the English in the management of their own lives would destroy the roots of national life. England would come to resemble a business corporation, he wrote: rights, duties and freedoms would be superseded by a universal obligation to serve the interests of the state.[22]

---

[18] *Liberties and Communities in Medieval England* by Helen Cam. Ironically, the most tyrannical of these administrations were called 'Liberties': there, nobles were given license to rule as they pleased subject to the terms of a grant from the monarch. Elsewhere, democracy and oligarchy, closed and open government, were in constant flux. An interesting addendum: for the continuity between the English parish vestry and the democratic town meeting in New England see: 'The Parish and the Town-Meeting' in White and Notestein, *Source Problems in English History* (1915), pp. 241 ff.

[19] An important essay on the continuity of self-government over many centuries is 'The Unacknowledged Republic: Officeholding in Early Modern England' by Mark Goldie in *The Politics of the Excluded* ed. Tim Harris (2001).

[20] See Chapter 3.

[21] Perhaps the most interesting English historians of local government reform are the Webbs (Sidney and Beatrice): intending to write a short book praising the reforms they ended up devoting much of their lives to researching and writing nine large volumes meticulously documenting what had been swept away.

[22] Gneist, *The History of the English Constitution* (London, 1891) p. 733; quoted by Bryan Keith-Lucas in *The Unreformed Local Government System* (1980) p. 91.

5. Freedom and democracy

Freedom and democracy are often talked about in the same breath as if they were an old and faithful married couple. It's well known that there are many meanings to the word 'freedom' and many of these are already recognized and established (to a degree) in the West: among them freedoms of speech, religion, association and movement. What kind of freedom would we expect democracy to add to these?

Probably the most significant democratic meaning of freedom is absence of privilege. Privilege allowed to one person is loss of freedom to another. The privileges which most characterise society under representative government are: the privileges of banks to manufacture money and for capitalists to use that money; the privilege of governments to create debt in the name of their citizens; the privileges of unaccountable officialdom which makes up its own rules; the privileges enjoyed by corporate personae over and above natural (human) persons. If these privileges were dispensed with, a kind of freedom would be born which today can only be read about in books.

6: How can 'the people' contribute to good government?

There are many objections to popular government, some rational and some pure bigotry or self-interest. In the past, objections were often written down at length[23] but deference to 'the people' is now obligatory in public and objections are more likely to be uttered in private. It is worth considering these objections before assessing the potential value of institutions of popular government.

The crudest and most obvious objection is that 'ordinary people' are generally less intelligent and competent than those who rise in the hierarchies of politics and power. This

---

[23]   Good examples are H.L. Mencken, *Notes on Democracy* and John Austin, *A Plea For The Constitution*. Many of the criticisms levelled against 'democracy' over the past two hundred years are in fact of course criticisms of representative government (which we have been lured into calling 'democracy'). Since the two types of government are very different, criticisms of one are likely to be irrelevant to the other.

may be countered by the observation that hypocrisy, ruthlessness, contempt for truth and an endless capacity for repetition seem to be more significant than intelligence and competence when it comes to success in political life. People not driven by ambition are more likely to want a congenial world; if politics is about living together, then ordinary concerns for fairness and justice are more valuable than the desire to steal a march on the other party.

Another objection is that many people are not interested in politics: they do not even bother to vote. Non-voters tend to be individuals who feel that no one represents their interests, so for them going to the polling booth would be a waste time. In more democratic systems, however, such as the Swiss, popular interest in politics is much greater.

Another objection is that popular decision-making is likely to be ill-informed and impulsive. Most people would agree that good decisions require careful consideration. It is perfectly possible to design institutions of popular government with this in mind. A typical example is the jury system in courts of law, where randomly-selected 'ordinary' citizens vote on the guilt or innocence of the accused after carefully hearing and considering the evidence and listening to the summing-up of an experienced judge. The result is reliable and conscientious justice. If readers of the national press, rather than jurors, were to vote on the guilt of the accused, the procedure would be grotesque.[24]

A fifth variety of objection is that government requires, like any art, familiarity and practice. This is undoubtedly true, and it is the main reason why governments rely on permanent staffers (civil servants) for day-to-day administration, advice and continuity etcetera.[25] Few people would suggest, for instance, that the transport system, or weapons procurement, be actually administered by randomly-

---

[24] It is, of course, possible to design or modify a jury system so that it resembles a farce, or is corruptible, or is amenable to political influence.

[25] Even in ancient Athens, the stability of government relied on civil servants (some of them slaves). See Hansen, *Athenian Democracy in the Age of Demosthenes* (1998), pp. 244, 342.

selected ordinary people; but public scrutiny and even deci-
sion-taking of both these activities might be better-made by
juries than by professional politicians.

One of the most interesting objections to 'the people' taking part in government is that they often prefer authorities
constituted on traditional, rather than rational, grounds. For
instance: How irrational it was, for the people of England to
prefer a monarchy to parliamentary government in the 17th
Century! — And to still want a monarch today, despite the
fact that the monarch is about as significant as a human tail
or appendix! Politicians and rationalists may despise ordinary people for being backward-looking; it may be, however, that 'the people' see through the claims of progress and
reason to the delusions and self-interest that lie beneath. Fur-
thermore, tradition can be more reliable than representation
when it comes to preserving rights and freedoms.[26]

7: *Constitutions, political institutions and democracy*

A constitution is the sum of laws and traditions which define
how a political community has come to rule itself or to be
ruled by others. Constitutions are normally defended against
impulsive change, but amenable to considered modification.
The importance for a country of its constitution — written or
unwritten — is hard to overestimate: it provides the framework in which lives are led, ambitions fulfilled or frustrated,
justice delivered or denied. A constitution moderates the
conditions of our lives in ways we hardly know.

A constitution cannot be meaningfully called 'democratic' unless it specifies a system or systems, commanding
force in law and practice, which enable ordinary people to
rule. This must include an element of sovereign power, such
as a binding veto exercised in referendum that can be triggered by popular initiative, not granted from above.

A political institution is essentially a system made real.
Electoral representation, for instance, is a system (citizens

---

[26]   See the way the House of Commons abolished rights of ordinary people
which had survived centuries of traditional government (Chapter 3).

choosing between would-be rulers) made real by people operating it, by buildings and other resources devoted to it, by specified events to trigger procedures, and (last but not least) constitutional authority which means its results will be binding.

There are a number of institutions which have some claim to being democratic (a brief summary of each follows this list): popular assemblies, assemblies selected by lot, rotation of office, 'scrutiny', office-holders selected by lot, the referendum, the initiative, and the power of recall. Unless the outcome of a democratic process is binding, it is not democratic: it is merely cosmetic or advisory.

Institutions of Democratic Government

1. *The citizens' assembly*

The citizens' assembly, in which members of a community come together to discuss matters that concern them all, is surely the earliest of all political forums. Its origins are lost in pre-history, but not hard to find in common sense: if there is trouble, the community gets together to sort it out.

According to Pierre Clastres, the politics of assemblies in simple (tribal) communities is designed to ward off hierarchy and to preserve equality.[27] Power is communal, vested in 'society', which consists of the traditions and habits of mind and behaviour of the tribe. 'The chief is there to serve society; it is society as such — the real locus of power — that exercises its authority over the chief.'[28] The principle of tribal government is to avoid the kind of power relations which characterise the state, by 'refusing to allow an individual, central, separate power to arise'.[29]

Among such communities there is a great deal of difference between tribes governed by men and tribes where

---

[27] Pierre Clastres died in 1977 at the age of 43. His two principal publications in English were *Society Against the State* (1977) and *The Archaeology of Violence* (posthumous, 2010).

[28] *Society Against the State*, p. 175.

[29] *Society Against the State*, p. 180.

property is predominantly owned by women (matrilineal or matriarchal societies).[30] The former rely on warfare for tribal stability; the latter upon conciliation, consensus and peaceful solutions. It is important to mention this for obvious reasons—warfare and competition for every type of power being the chief threats to the continued existence of the human race. The study of matriarchal societies has been mostly treated with dismissal and contempt by the academic world, perhaps because it calls into question the fundamental assumptions of several thousand years of Western civilization. With increasing involvement of women in all areas of public life, however, practical reality is moving ahead regardless of academic understanding (or lack of it). (There is, of course, a difference between the kind of success enjoyed by women who have to compete in a man's world and the kind of authority which sustains matrilineal societies.)

In the male-dominated historical mainstream of Western civilization, complex societies—hierarchical and internally specialised—developed through several kinds of process: the coming together of tribes, the conquest by one people of another, migrations and sheer growth in size. It was the achievement of certain Greek city states to develop institutions of democracy which could function in more complex states, enabling 'the people' to resist domination by one person or by an exclusive few.

The general assembly was the most basic and simple of these, and decisions taken there had the kind of authority that today we would call 'sovereign'. All citizens were enti-

---

[30]   'Matrilineal' means that property is carried in the female line; matriarchy traditionally means 'rule by the motherhood'. However, Heide Goettner-Abendroth (*Matriarchal Societies*, 2012) and Peggy Reeves Sanday (*Women at the Center: Life in a Modern Matriarchy*, 2003) characterise matriarchies as societies not built on domination by women (i.e. not mirror images of patriarchy) but on values of equality and consensus. *Beyond Adversary Democracy* by Jane Mansbridge (1981) is a more general study of assemblies as methods of reaching consensus.

tled to attend, and the assembly reached decisions by a public show of hands following open discussion.[31]

In ancient Greece, women and slaves were excluded from citizenship and therefore from citizens' assemblies, which were regarded as democratic nevertheless when they included the poor. The poor were always a majority, so in a democracy they were understood to be the politically dominant class. When they decided in the common interest, it was *good* democracy; when they decided in their own interest—to rob the rich, perhaps, and throw them out of the city—it was *bad* democracy.

Citizens' assemblies survive to the present day, most famously in Swiss communes and cantons, and in townships in New England in the USA. Switzerland is an interesting case, as it is the only modern state to have preserved systems of democracy at all levels of political activity. Its constitution, which has evolved over a thousand years and counting, has 'not just one or two unusual structures but a whole constellation of them.'[32] The political arrangements of Switzerland are (or should be) a resource-book for ideas on democracy.[33] Just as the Greeks invented institutions so that democracy could operate within the city state, so the Swiss developed institutions which enabled democracy to operate within the nation state (some of these are addressed later in this chapter).[34]

---

[31]   Hansen, *Athenian Democracy in the Age of Demosthenes* (1998) gives an extremely good overview of democratic institutions and their development. The Athenian constitution changed over time and the generalisations made here do not apply to the whole timescale of 'Athenian democracy'.

[32]   Clive Church, *The Politics and Government of Switzerland* (2004), p. 181.

[33]   Among other interesting books on Swiss politics: *Modern Democracies* by James Bryce (1921); Wolf Linder, *Swiss Democracy* (1994); Benjamin Barber, *The Death of Communal Liberty* (1974), Jonathan Steinberg *Why Switzerland?*(1996); Kris Kobach, *The Referendum: Direct Democracy in Switzerland* (1993).

[34]   The story of how national democracy developed in Switzerland but was defeated in the rest of Europe is told in *The Medieval City State* (1926) by Maude V. Clarke.

The full citizens' assembly in Switzerland is in use today
at the lower levels of government (the communes) and also
at higher level in two small cantons, both with less than
40,000 inhabitants.[35] Citizens' assemblies are the bedrock of
the Swiss constitution and great deference is paid to them.
The 3,000 communes have 'a constitutional right to exist
which cannot be withdrawn... this means that a reform of
local government "from above" would be impossible in
Switzerland.'[36]

The independence of the communes and the device of
the referendum (see later) ensure that in Switzerland 'sovereignty' — the final say in what happens — lies with the people,
not just in theory but also in reality. The 'consent of the people' is not the passive consent of a dog lying down in sub-
mission: it is an active procedure, of acceptance or denial
and of demands initiated among the people which, if a majority rules in their favour, are binding upon the government.[37] In the words of Thomas Fleiner, 'The Confederation
of Switzerland is not a decentralised State giving authority to
the cantons, it is a State which derives its power from the
consent of the cantons and of the people.'[38]

The town meetings of New England in the United States
are another survival of the citizens' assembly. From a very
interesting book on the subject (*Real Democracy* by Frank M.
Bryan):

> In America, town meeting predates representative government.
> It is stitched into the fabric of New England and dominates the
> patchwork of its public past. ... It is accessible to every citizen,
> coded in law, and conducted regularly in over 1,000 towns.[39]

---

[35] These are Appenzell Innerrhoden and Glarus. Images and videos are
available on the web.

[36] Wolf Linder, *Swiss Democracy* (1994), p. 49.

[37] A majority of citizens and of cantons, which gives country-dwellers
equal influence with cities.

[38] 'The Concept of the Constitution of Switzerland' (Kleine Institutsreihe
Nr. 7, 1983) p. 10.

[39] Frank M. Bryan, *Real Democracy: The New England Town Meeting and How
It Works* (Chicago U.P. 2004) page 3.

Bryan adds the curious fact that while a whole industry of students and professors investigates the democracy of ancient Athens, functioning democracy in the United States is almost entirely ignored by academics of political science.

Town meetings are sovereign over local matters: their powers vary greatly from one place to another, and may include such items as budget and taxation, electing local officers, highway construction, issuing licenses and overseeing town activities. On occasion they play a part in larger affairs. The whole of America sat up, took notice (and fell in line) when a town meeting passed a motion that the President of the United States should be impeached.[40]

Face-to-face assemblies of ALL citizens are obviously impracticable when hundreds of thousands—let alone millions—of citizens are involved. Mechanisms which enable larger populations to vote on single issues (referenda, initiatives, recall) will be mentioned later in this chapter. The face-to-face nature of a citizens' assembly, however, makes it a uniquely valuable device, without which other forms of democracy must lose some of their meaning. If the decisions of a citizens' assembly are significant and binding, there will be a strong incentive for people to participate; if it is used in coordination with other democratic mechanisms, such as rotation and election to higher-level assemblies, it is a powerful instrument of self-government.

On matters of state or national importance (for instance reform of the constitution), it would be perfectly possible for citizens' assemblies to meet simultaneously across a state or nation, and the results be collated. Face-to-face discussion and consideration would lead to a more considered democratic decision than might be expected, say, from a referendum.

As always, there is no sense in such meetings unless the decisions taken are binding. Otherwise they are futile and cynical exercises conducted for the benefit of those who hold real power—either cosmetic, or testing the water to see what

---

[40] The town meeting was in Thetford, Vermont in 1974; the President was Nixon: he resigned on August 9th to avoid impeachment.

can be gotten away with, or attempts to palliate the anger of citizens.

2: Assemblies chosen by lot

A jury is a group of citizens selected by lot.[41] Today, juries are most familiar in the context of criminal trials but in the past, groups of citizens chosen by lot exercised political power as well as judicial power. There are movements afoot today to re-introduce this practice.[42]

The most famous use of political and administrative juries was again in ancient Athens.[43] The *boule* (council) consisted of 500 citizens chosen by lot. Not only did the *boule* decide what questions should be put to the citizens' assembly; it was also responsible for making sure that decisions, once taken, were put into practice.

Because it met every weekday and took up someone's life for a whole year, the *boule* was selected from citizens who both put themselves forward and were approved by their local neighbourhoods.[44] To preserve its character as a group of ordinary citizens, and to discourage the growth of power and influence (factions), individuals could serve only once or at most twice. Hansen estimates that two-thirds of Athenian citizens over forty would have served in the *boule*.[45]

Athenians made a distinction between laws and decrees: laws were more permanent (for instance laws on murder or inheritance), while decrees were things used up once they

---

[41]   The word 'jury' comes from the swearing-in process (*jurée*) which commits someone chosen for a purpose to acting truthfully and honourably.

[42]   Different terminologies are used in different proposals for assemblies chosen by lot. For instance 'mini-publics' and 'mini-populi' for the assemblies; 'sortition' for the process of selection by lot; 'demarchy' and 'lottocracy' for government by lot-selected assembly.

[43]   Mogens Herman Hansen in *Athenian Democracy in the Age of Demosthenes* (2nd ed. 1999) provides a meticulous description of what is known of political institutions and procedures.

[44]   See Hansen, p. 248. Hansen speculates that sometimes moral pressure must have been brought to bear on individuals to serve.

[45]   Hansen, p. 249.

were implemented (for instance, a decision to go to war or to share out the spoils of war). The assembly of all citizens made decrees: the procedure for making changes in the law was more complicated (and it changed considerably over time). Generally, proposals could come from almost anywhere including the individual citizen (*ho boulomenos*, 'he who wishes', the ultimate political actor in the city-state). Proposals were passed back and forth between assemblies for modification and approval or rejection, before being finally literally 'written in stone' and put on public display.[46]

The *boule* was the most important of many groups of citizens selected by lot.

In the law courts no professionals took part, although professional speech-writers could be hired to write speeches. Each side presented its case, the jury listened and decided. Today we are used to juries consisting of twelve people, but in ancient Athens they generally consisted of hundreds of citizens, and in important cases of a thousand or more. This meant that almost all citizens were called on to serve their country in some capacity many times during a normal lifetime.

The courts themselves exercised functions we would now call 'political': in Hansen's words, they 'had unlimited power to control the Assembly, the Council, the magistrates and the political leaders'.[47] They also had administrative responsibilities, overseeing public expenditures and dealing with citizens' objections. In these committee-style juries, citizens served much shorter terms, making it easier for people to fit political activity into their normal lives.

The versatility and potential of bodies of citizens chosen at random to exercising public responsibility can hardly be exaggerated. Even today, most citizens—including ones reduced to apathy by years or even generations of subjection—

---

46   Hansen, pp 161-177.
47   Hansen, p. 179.

act with a sense of purpose and communal responsibility when it is required of them.[48]

Assemblies chosen by lot were regarded as democratic if they were selected from among *all* citizens and if they recognised the general assembly of all citizens as a superior authority. If an assembly was chosen from a privileged group—from the wealthy, perhaps, or from a limited number of families—then it was regarded as oligarchic. If it was merely the obedient underling to a tyrant it was, of course, the very opposite of 'democratic'.

Political assemblies selected by lot continued to feature in European life in all three categories: democracy, oligarchy and tyranny. In later history, they were most often *not* democratic: the pool of citizens from which jurors were chosen tended to exclude the poor, or be restricted to members of a particular party or to a few families.[49] Their use is documented in hundreds of towns and cities of the Middle Ages and Renaissance, and in some cases the practice survived into the 19th century.[50]

An interesting suggestion concerning how juries might make political decisions today reflects how they are used in courts of law. Keith Sutherland's *A People's Parliament* outlines a system for a legislative chamber selected by lot. Arguments concerning the pros and cons of a particular proposal are put by professional advocates to the assembly, which then votes upon both policy and changes to the law.[51]

---

[48]   *Petite histoire de l'experimentation democratique* by Yves Sintomer (2011), shortly to be published in English translation by Imprint Academic, gives many examples.

[49]   Putting into practice a principle noted in the Bible: 'The lot causeth contentions to cease / And between the mighty it separateth' (Proverbs 18,18).

[50]   *Medieval City States* by Maude V. Clarke (1926) surveys the political history and development of these states. Histories of individual cities such as *History of Lucca* (John Jones, 2010) or *A History of Siena* (Langton Douglas, 1902) give a good idea of the context in which these mechanisms of government developed.

[51]   *A People's Parliament* by Keith Sutherland, Imprint Academic (2008). Imprint Academic is publishing a series of book on 'sortition' — the po-

3: Office-holders chosen by lot

In Athens, most state officials (or magistrates) were chosen by lot: only where special competence was required, such as in military command, was election preferred as a method of choice. The democratic significance is obvious: lot drew virtually all citizens into holding some kind of office and so fulfilled the ideal of democracy in practice, which was 'to rule and be ruled in turn.'[52]

The drawbacks are equally obvious. Few things are worse than finding oneself at the mercy of an official who is incompetent, bloody-minded, corrupt, or stark-staring mad. The Athenians coped with this problem partly by a process of scrutiny before confirming the official appointment (see later in this chapter); and partly by making sure that (as far as possible) officials operated in groups of ten. To us, the idea of negotiating with a group of ten over, say, a bathroom extension is very foreign, but presumably this was a familiar part of ancient Greek life: the Chorus in Greek drama seems more understandable in the light of it. The collegial character of officialdom also prevented any one person from acquiring too much power or influence; bribery became expensive, complicated and more likely to be detected and reported.[53]

Selection of office-holders by lot may be used also for purposes not at all democratic. An example of non-democratic use is when lucrative offices, such as collecting taxes from subject populations, were divvied up among members of an oligarchy, such as happened in certain city-states (Bologna, Pisa) during the Middle Ages.[54]

---

litical potential of selection by lot. See also *The Athenian Option* by Anthony Barnett and Peter Carty (same publisher).

[52] Aristotle, *Politics* Bk 6 Ch 2 (1317b2-3).

[53] Hansen, *Athenian Democracy in the Age of Demosthenes,* p. 237. Hansen also mentions that continuity and competence were probably supplied by the secretaries to the magistrates (perhaps as Jeeves supplied common sense to Wooster).

[54] *The City-State in Europe* by Tom Scott (2012), p. 42.

4: Rotation of office

Rotation of office means that individual citizens take it in turns to fulfil various duties. This might be at village level, where duties such as keeping the footpaths clear, making sure the beer is properly brewed and the post of village constable are passed along a rota of villagers; or it might be at the highest level, as with the office of Head-of-State in both ancient Greece and present-day Switzerland.[55] Switzerland has four official languages; most citizens are multilingual, and rotating the office of Head-of-State helps keep a degree of respect and familiarity between the different linguistic communities.

In ancient Greece, rotation of office was used to include everyone in practical political responsibility. You were a citizen to the extent that you enjoyed rights of participation, including holding office.[56] Rotation was often used together with selection by lot: for instance, the *boule,* selected by lot, was divided into ten groups, each of which in rotation served for a period of 35 or 36 days as the executive committee.

5: Referenda, initiatives and recalls

The referendum is a system that allows the whole citizen body to vote and decide on a certain issue. Obviously this has become a much easier and more practicable process since the advent of electronic means of communication, in particular the internet. To what extent, and in what form, is it desirable?

---

[55] In ancient Athens 'every fourth adult male Athenian citizen could say 'I have been for twenty-four hours President of Athens''' (Hansen, p. 314). In modern-day Switzerland the office is more restricted: it rotates among the members of the Federal Council in order of seniority (Wikipedia article 'President of the Swiss Confederation' accessed 21/09/2012. Formally, the post is elected, but the tradition as outlined above is always followed.)

[56] Aristotle *Politics* Book 3 Chapter 1 (1275b).

In Switzerland, the referendum was instituted at national level in 1848 after centuries of use at lower levels.[57] Referenda are binding and can be initiated fairly easily by groups of citizens (currently 50,000 signatures gathered within a hundred days). Almost any decision made by the government can be revoked by a popular referendum, and the political elite avoids doing something which would provoke a referendum.[58] This is frustrating for ambitious politicians with big plans, but it preserves democracy.

The referendum, like any political institution, can be well or badly designed. Its character as a democratic instrument may be undermined by undemocratic powers: perhaps the most grotesque example of this is in the United States of America where the Supreme Court has upheld the right of corporations to initiate state-level referenda as if they were human citizens. The outcome is another wrench away from democracy towards commercial corporate power.[59] There is no provision at all for holding referenda at the federal level in the United States. (In the United States, a referendum triggered by citizens' petition is called an 'initiative'.)

Most observers agree that Swiss provisions for several types of referendum, triggered either by popular demand or automatically for constitutional proposals, work well even if some of the decisions are not approved by those who set themselves up as moral authorities.[60] An interesting aspect of Swiss usage is that once a referendum is triggered, the legislature has the opportunity to prepare a counter-proposal. The counter-proposal is often a more considered and workable version of the initiative itself, in which case

---

[57] Kris Kobach, *The Referendum: Direct Democracy in Switzerland* (1993). This book, by someone who has become a controversial U.S. politician, is in very few libraries and extremely hard to find.

[58] Preface to *Swiss Constitutional Law* by Thomas Fleiner, Alexander Misic and Nicole Toepperwien (Dike, 2005).

[59] *The Economist* (April 20th 2011) contained a special report comparing use of referenda in Switzerland and California.

[60] Anti-democrats posing as moralists pounce with glee on decisions that seem illiberal; in reality, however, decisions are usually both liberal and conservative in ethos.

voters have two versions of proposed new legislation to choose from.

Obviously the device of the referendum is not democratic if it can only be triggered by government decision, if the government is in charge of the wording, or if the result is not binding. The government of the UK has recently introduced one of the more transparent exercises in fake democracy. Called an 'e-petition' (a petition is a plea to a deity) it is a plea to the government to consider holding a debate about doing something. If a petition 'gets at least 100,000 signatures, it will be considered for debate in the House of Commons'.[61] It is, however, welcomed by some practical democrats as a 'foot in the door'.

The device known as 'recall' is 'a procedure by which voters can remove an elected official from office through a direct vote before his or her term has ended' (Wikipedia definition). As a practical restraint on the behaviour of elected officials, provision for a recall would seem to be both a good and democratic idea. It is related to the next democratic procedure to be considered: the scrutiny.

6: The scrutiny[62]

The scrutiny is a simple mechanism to ensure accountability in office. It consists of investigations into a person's character and behaviour before and after they take office. Before they take office, a jury assesses whether they satisfy the qualifications: Is the person a citizen? Of the right age? Not a criminal? Not insane? After a period in office, another jury conducts an investigation into whether the official has conducted his or herself honourably (not taking bribes, betraying the common interest, etcetera). Any citizen may lodge a complaint against an official, and that complaint must be investigated during the scrutiny process (there are penalties for citizens who make malicious or unjustified complaints).

---

[61] http://epetitions.direct.gov.uk/ 04/10/2012.
[62] Here I use the term to include both the *squittino* associated with medieval city-states and the before-and-after practices called *Dokimasia* and *Euthynai* in ancient Greek democracy.

The abandonment of any kind of scrutiny is an obvious symptom of surrender to elitism and privilege. Its revived use would be devastating to the corrupt elites which run many countries today as their milch-cows. It would also draw attention to the systemic privilege in money and finance, which has been effectively hidden from popular notice now for over two hundred years. It is inconceivable that democratic scrutiny would allow the kind of financial arrangements discussed in Chapter 4.

In democratic societies, duties are undertaken voluntarily and for minimal pay, and scrutiny of officials has been common practice. In representative government, where career politicians take high salaries and top them up with manifold perks of office, it is left to the media (when so inclined) to ferret out abuse. It might seem strange that salaried officials are today largely immune to popular account, when unpaid volunteer politicians in democracies were dragged through public scrutiny. Historically, however, this is not hard to understand. Sir Lewis Namier, the great historian of the early days of representative government in England wrote: 'Men… no more dreamt of a seat in the House in order to benefit humanity than a child dreams of a birthday-cake that others may eat it.'[63] He adds: 'which is perfectly normal and in no way reprehensible': meaning, (I presume) that representatives are human; what else do we expect of them?

Summary

It is hard to exaggerate the perilous state of the world after two centuries of government by electoral representation. The present (2013) financial crisis is merely the tip of an iceberg. Power lies with governments which claim to be rational and progressive, but which promote war, pollution, waste, environmental destruction and the transfer of assets to an unaccountable and irresponsible minority. The ideals of freedom and democracy have been betrayed: countless lives are in

---

[63] The Structure Of Politics At The Accession Of George III (1957), p. 2.

thrall to systems designed and administered in secret. When farms, houses, businesses, jobs, belongings, livelihoods and lives are lost to an immense and parasitical plutocracy, what else can be recommended besides a dose of democracy? A dose may be momentary—a reminder by riot or rebellion to those who rule; or it may be ongoing and constitutional. The story is hardly new—it is as old as civilization itself.

How realistic is it to think we might see developments of true constitutional democracy? Many think this is close to inconceivable: 'the people' are happy to leave politicising to others, and elites are naturally opposed to fundamental change. However, a number of efforts are under way to introduce democratic practices into our modern world. If a popular appetite for democracy—for political responsibility and freedom—appeared, then things could change very fast.[64]

In South America, the Porto Alegre experiment in 'participatory budgeting' has received great publicity. 'Participatory budgeting' means bringing citizens together to decide what tax-money should be spent on, with officials and experts on hand, not to make decisions but to assist. Porto Alegre is a city of 1.5 million people. Perhaps most interestingly of all, during this experiment 'Tax evasion fell, as people saw what their money was being spent on.'[65] Democracy is inspiring. More than 200 cities across the world have since initiated their own versions of 'Porto Alegre democracy'.[66]

In 2005, the academic and activist James Fishkin was invited to introduce decision-making by political jury at a local level in China.[67] The idea was to bring together 'a random sample of citizens to create a microcosm of the public who can deliberate together and become more informed, and then express their views on behalf of the rest of the citi-

---

[64]   Graham Smith, *Democratic Innovations* (2009) is an academic overview.

[65]   Patrick Kingsley in The Guardian, 10/09/12.

[66]   There are many books on the subject. Iain Bruce's *The Porto Alegre Alternative* (2004) contains English translations of essays and interviews with the experiment's creators: others in English are by Gianpaolo Baiocchi (2005) and Marion Gret and Yves Sintomer (2005).

[67]   James S. Fishkin, *When the People Speak* (2011).

zenry.'[68] Western commentators, accustomed to believing themselves genuine monopolists of democracy, appeared somewhat miffed at the Chinese Communist Party apparently promoting democracy. The Chinese explanation: 'The local government needed deliberative and consultative meetings to reduce conflicts of interest, reduce any perception of corruption, and provide a channel for citizens and interest groups to express their concerns about municipal construction projects.'[69]

In British Columbia, a Canadian province, an assembly of citizens chosen by lot, jury-style, formulated a recommendation for electoral reform. Their rather tame recommendation was defeated in a referendum. These are early days.

Experiments continue with referenda, initiatives and recall in the US and in Europe: two publications and an institute provide updates on developments and the practical implications of how they are instituted and designed.[70]

Communities run on democratic lines in Europe are seedlings which could propagate. Christiania in Denmark is one of the most established. From a guide book to Copenhagen: 'More so than in the polis of ancient Athens, government (*of Christiania*) is fully democratic and all major decisions are reached at open meetings to which everyone living in Christiania is invited. When a general meeting is in progress, the shops and cafes close down and discussion of items on the agenda continue until a consensus is reached. Decisions are not made on the basis of voting and, consequently, decisions are not arrived at quickly. The town is broken down into 15 administrative and autonomous districts that hold their own monthly meetings, and contact groups are formed by district representatives as and when the need arises.'[71]

---

[68] Interview, http://www.re-public.gr/en/?p=58 (accessed 28/12/12).
[69] http://cdd.stanford.edu/polls/china/ (accessed 28/12/12)
[70] *The Initiative and Referendum Almanac* and *Direct Democracy in Europe*, both sponsored by the I&R Institute http://www.iandrinstitute.org/ (University of Southern California) which is dedicated to the study of referendums and initiatives.
[71] Sean Sheehan, *Copenhagen* (2003). Sometimes the Danish government tries to suppress Christiania, but a majority of Danes are in favour of let-

Cooperative movements around the world have evolved decision-making processes with political potential (sociocracy has already been mentioned). In a sense, the cooperative movement is democracy invading business; a re-invasion back would involve incorporating some democratic practices, especially the generation of ideas 'from below', into politics.[72] Again, this could be either a meaningless (palliative) exercise imposed top-down or part of a binding and truly democratic political structure.

Working examples of democracy are evidence that true democracy is viable in the modern age. The survival of representative government in England, long after it had been suppressed elsewhere in Europe, inspired a revival of representative government in the 18th and 19th centuries: in a similar manner, survivals of true democracy are already inspiring a democratic revival two-and-a-half thousand years after its debut in ancient Greece.

On the negative side, many people do not know that there are democratic alternatives to electoral representation. Others believe that politics should be entrusted to 'experts'. Still others seem content to relinquish political freedom and responsibility in exchange for trickle-down consumer comforts. Only when the greed of the privileged seems about to devour everything, are such assumptions and arrangements threatened.[73]

On the other hand, communities with established traditions of democracy have defended their ways of life, sometimes to death or extinction. In Switzerland, communes in the valleys and mountains defended democratic institutions

---

ting it be. In 1996 a poll was taken: 60% of Danes wanted it protected; 20% wanted it closed down.

[72] Richard C. Williams, *The Cooperative Movement: Globalization from Below* (2007).

[73] Privileged elites have a habit of pushing things too far: in Adam Smith's words '"All for ourselves and nothing for other people" seems, in every age of the world, to have been the vile maxim of the masters of mankind.' *Wealth of Nations* (Glasgow Edition, OUP) Book III, Chapter IV, p. 448.

against the oligarchic tendencies of the cities and also against foreign invasion.[74] But how have new democracies arisen?

Revolutions have not, in modern times, ushered in democracy. Managed by intellectuals and activists, they have installed new oligarchies, composed initially of the revolutionaries themselves. In the words of Franz Kafka: 'The Revolution evaporates and leaves behind only the slime of a new bureaucracy. The chains of tormented mankind today are made of red tape.'[75]

Democratic constitutions have always been more complex than the formulaic constitutions of electoral representation, and also more amenable to change, evolving slowly by experience of what works. In the past, new democracies have arisen when the efforts of individuals and popular inclinations coincided, and combined to give a practical outcome.[76] It seems that certain influential individuals have preferred to institute democracy even when they have had the opportunity to seize power for themselves.[77] The human impulse to live in freedom has always competed with the

---

[74]   Napoleon's attempt to impose representative government upon Switzerland (1798) met various degrees of resistance from democratic communities. 'In September, tiny Nidwalden rose in resistance. In the resulting battle against French forces vastly superior in number, every farm was transformed into a fortress. A slaughter ensued in which 400 of the canton's inhabitants were killed, nearly one third of them women and children. Although the rebellion was ultimately quashed, it cost the lives of more than 2,000 French soldiers.' Kris W. Kobach, *The History of Direct Democracy in Switzerland*. No one knows how many self-governing polities were obliterated, two thousand years earlier, by Alexander the Great.

[75]   Gustav Janouch, *Conversations with Kafka* (2nd ed. 1971), p. 120.

[76]   Democracy in ancient Athens was instituted gradually, over a period of a hundred years or more, as a succession of individuals made changes which 'the people'—expressing their decision sometimes in violence and riot—welcomed and accepted. In Rhode Island, the democratic Charters of 1647 and 1663 were carried by the efforts of individuals—Roger Williams and John Clarke—embodying the preferences of many who had settled there in hope of religious freedom, democracy, and respect for indigenous Americans.

[77]   In Athens: Solon, Cleisthenes; in Rhode Island: Roger Williams and John Clarke.

impulse to power, both within individuals and in society outside.

The arrival of the internet has seemed to open up possibilities for political change. Information and opinion can travel faster than ever before; but the sheer volume of material means that, as before, people seek out what they want to find. It is true that the Arab Spring spread like wildfire with the help of the internet; but on the other hand, revolution in Europe way back in 1848 spread only a little more slowly.

It remains to be seen whether the internet will be the seedbed of new political thought and action, or just another place where minorities let off steam. In representative government, the mainstream is the source of power. Dissident minorities are (mostly) tolerated. The internet is a forum for ideas and debate, but it is also a place (as events in many parts of the world have already proved) where individuals may be identified, tracked down and eliminated.

The internet has become yet another battleground where freedom of expression must be preserved against the great corporate interests of state and commerce. The true contribution of the internet is perhaps that its structure makes it harder for power to coax, crush and mould opinion into its own favoured image: only time will tell.

The democratic procedures outlined in this chapter are a cornucopia of opportunities. The most urgently-needed innovation would seem to be some kind of scrutiny of money-creation (see Chapter Four). The most promising introductions in terms of good government must vary from place to place; in some places the scrutiny, in others political assemblies selected by lot, in others concerted citizens' assemblies, in others referenda and initiatives. The spirit of democracy, which has kept a low profile for two-and-a-half thousand years now, inspires people to evolve their own forms of self-government, not to accept them ready-made. Perhaps, as the spirit of democracy re-establishes itself in the world, constitutions will arise that enable communities to live in peace, both internally and with each other.

Or at any rate, a bit more so.

SELECT BIBLIOGRAPHY

Many texts, particularly classics, are available free online at sites such as The Internet Archive, Project Gutenberg, Liberty Fund and Mises.org.

Acton, John Dalberg (Lord). *Lectures on the French Revolution*, Liberty Fund, available online; *Letters to Mary Gladstone* (1913); 'Sir Erskine May's Democracy in Europe', in *The History of Freedom and Other Essays* (1922); 'The Rise of the Whigs' and 'The Puritan Revolution' in *Lectures in Modern History* (1906).

Allais, Maurice. La Crise mondiale d'aujourd'hui. Pour de profondes réformes des institutions financières et monétaires, 1999. Also article in Marianne, December 11, 2009.

Allen, J.W. A History of Political Thought in the Sixteenth Century (1957).

Arendt, Hannah. *On Revolution* (1963).

Aristotle. *Politics* tr. Sinclair, ed. Saunders (2000); *Nicomachean Ethics* tr. Thomson, Tredennick, ed. Barnes (2004).

Arnold, Thurman W. (ed) The Future Of Democratic Capitalism (1950).

D'Argenson, Marquis Considérations Sur le Government Ancien et Present de la France (1764).

Austin, John. A Plea for the Constitution (1859).

Ashley, Sir William. The Economic Organisation of England (1914, 1957).

Baer, Peter. 'Black Africa: the Living Legacy of Dying Colonialism' in *Reality and Rhetoric* (1984), pp 90-105; 'Broadcasting the Liberal Death Wish' in *Equality, The Third World and Economic Delusion* (1981).

Barante, Baron de. La Vie Politique de Monsieur Royer-Collard (1861).

Barber, Benjamin. The Death of Communal Liberty: A History of Freedom in a Swiss Mountain Canton (1974).

Barkai, Avraham. *Nazi Economics* (1990).

Barnett, Anthony and Carty, Peter. *The Athenian Option* (2008).

Barrow, G.W.S. *Feudal Britain* (1962).

Baster, A.S.J. *The International Banks* (1935,1977).

Beard Charles A. An Economic Interpretation of the Constitution of the United States (1913); The Republic (1943).

Beresford, Maurice. *The Lost Villages of England* (1998).

Berle, A. & Means, G. The Modern Corporation and Private Property (1932).

Bharata. *Natya Shastra* (date uncertain).

Birks, Peter. *Unjust Enrichment* (2005).

Blum, William. Rogue Nation (2002) Killing Hope (2003) and Freeing the World to Death (2004).

Bodin, Jean. *The Six Bookes of a Commonweale,* trans. Richard Knolles (1962).

Boeke, Kees. *Sociocracy,* available for download online.

Borio, C. and Disyatat, P. 'Global imbalances and the financial crisis: Link or no link?' Bank for International Settlements, Working Paper No 346. Available online.

Bouvier, John. A Law Dictionary, Adapted to the Constitution and Laws of the United States, 1856.

Bradlee, Helen West. A Student's Course On Legal History (1929).

Bruce, Iain (ed & tr). The Porto Alegre Alternative: Direct Democracy in Action (2011).

Bryan, Frank M. Real Democracy: The New England Town Meeting and How It Works (2004).

Bryce, James. *Modern Democracies* (1921).

Burckhardt, Jacob. Reflections on History and Judgements on History and Historians (both available online at Liberty Fund); History of Greek Culture (1963); The Greeks and Greek Civilization (1998).

Cam, Helen. Liberties and Communities in Medieval England (1944).

Cambridge Modern History Vol. X: *The French Revolution* (1907).

Cappon, Lester (ed.). *The Adams-Jefferson Letters: The Complete Correspondence Between Thomas Jefferson and Abigail and John Adams* (2008).

Carus-Wilson, Eleonora M. (ed.). *Essays in Economic History Vols I-III* (1954-62).

Chapman, John. 'The Extent and Nature of Parliamentary Enclosure', *Agricultural History Review*, XXXV, 1 (1987).

Charlesworth, John. The Principles of Company Law (1932).

Chinweizu. Voices from Twentieth-Century Africa (1988).

Chomsky, Noam. Profit over People: Neoliberalism and Global Order (1998).

Chua, Amy. *The World on Fire* (2003).

Clarke, Maud V. Medieval Representation and Consent (1936, 1964); The Medieval City State (1966).

Clastres, Pierre. Society Against the State (1977) and The Archaeology of Violence (posthumous, 2010).

Cobb, Richard and Jones, Colin. The French Revolution: Voices from a Momentous Epoch (1988).

Cooke, C.A. Corporation, Trust and Company (1950).

Craiutu, Aurelian. Liberalism under Siege: The Political Thought of the French Doctrinaires (2003).

Crick, F.W. 'The Genesis of Bank Deposits' *Economica* 7 (1927); *A Hundred Years of Joint Stock Banking* (1936).

Darlington, C.D. The Evolution of Man and Society (1969).

Darwin, Charles. *The Descent of Man* (1871) available online.

Davies, Bill. 'More Than the Bottom Line', *New Law Journal*, 158, Issue 7331, 2008.

Debord, Guy. Comments on the Society of the Spectacle (1988).

Defoe, Daniel. *History of the Last Four Years of the Queen* (pub. 1758) available online.

De Roover, Raymond. Business, Banking and Economic Thought in Late Mediaeval and Early Modern Europe (1976).

Dicey, A.V. Law and Opinion in England (1914).

Dickinson, H.T. *Liberty and Property* (1979).

Dickson, P.G.M. The Financial Revolution in England (1967).

Drucker, P. A Functioning Society (2003).

Eggert, Kurt. 'Held Up In Due Course', *Creighton Law Review*, Vol. 35 (2002).

Ernst, Morris. 'The Preservation of Civil Liberties' in *The Future of Democratic Capitalism* ed. Thurman Arnold (1950).

Feavearyear A., *The Pound Sterling* (1931, 1963).

Fetter, F.W. The Development of British Monetary Orthodoxy (1965).

Finer, S.E. The History of Government (1997).

Fischer, David. The Revolution of American Conservatism (1969).

Fisher, Irving. *100% Money* (1935).

Fishkin, James S. *When the People Speak* (2011).

Fleiner, Misic and Toepperwien. *Swiss Constitutional Law* (2005).

Ford, Henry J. Representative Government (1924).

Freeman, J. The Growth of The English Constitution (1876).

Friedman, M. 'A Monetary and Fiscal Framework for Economic Stability' in *The American Economic Review*, Vol. 38, No. 3.

Galbraith, J.K. Money: Whence It Came, Where It Went (1977); The New Industrial State (1967); The Economics of Innocent Fraud (2004).

Gardiner, S.R. *The Constitutional Documents of the Puritan Revolution* (1906) available online at Internet Archive.

Gneist, Rudolf. The English Parliament (1886), The History of the English Constitution (1891).

Goettner-Abendroth, Heide. *Matriarchal Societies* (2012).

Goldie, Mark. 'The Unacknowledged Republic: Officeholding in Early Modern England' in *The Politics of the Excluded* ed. Tim Harris (2001).

Gray, Alexander. The Development of Economic Doctrine (1933).

Gray, John. Black Mass (2008), Straw Dogs (2003) and False Dawn (2009).

Guéniffey, P. Le Nombre et La Raison (1993).

Guizot, François. *The Origins of Representative Government* (1854: translation available online at Liberty Fund); 'De la démocratie dans les sociétés modernes' (pamphlet) 1838; *Democracy in France* (1848).

Hammond, John and Barbara. The Village Labourer 1760-1832: a Study of the Government of England before the Reform Bill (1911), The Town Labourer 1760-1832: The New Civilisation (1917) and The Skilled Labourer 1760-1832 (1919)

Hampton, C. (ed.). *A Radical Reader* (2006).

Hansen, M.H. *The Athenian Democracy in the Age of Demosthenes* (1998); 'The mixed constitution versus the separation of powers: Monarchical and aristocratic aspects of modern democracy', History of Political Thought, XXXI, 2010.

Hennessy, Peter. *The Prime Minister* (2001).

Hiatt, Steven, ed. *A Game As Old As Empire* (2007).

Hobbes, Thomas. *Leviathan* (1651).

Holdsworth. *A History of English Law*. Many editions: the period during which credit creation was legitimised is well covered in the relevant volume.

Homer, Sidney. A History of Interest Rates (1977).

Horsefield, Keith. British Monetary Experiments 1650-1710 (1960).

Huerta de Soto, Jesus. *Money, Bank Credit and Economic Cycles.* Available online.

Humphrey, Thomas M. 'The Theory Of Multiple Expansion Of Deposits: What It Is And Whence It Came' in *Economic Review* March/April 1987. Available online at the Federal Bank of Richmond website.

Hunt, B.C. The Development of the Business Corporation in England, 1800-1867 (1936).

Johnson, Paul. *Making the Market* (2010).

Jones, Michae., Creative Accounting, Fraud and International Accounting Scandals (2010).

Kansu, Aykut. The Revolution of 1908 in Turkey (1997).

Keith-Lucas, Bryan. Unreformed Local Government (1979).

Kennan, George. *American Diplomacy* (1951, 2012).

Kern, Fritz. Kingship and Law in the Middle Ages (1968).

Keynes, John Maynard. 'The Economic Consequences of the Peace (1919), available online at Project Gutenberg; *A Treatise on Money* (1930, 2011).

King, Mervyn. 'Speech to the Buttonwood Gathering, New York, 25 October 2010' available online on the Bank of England website.

Kinzer, Stephen. *Overthrow* (2006); *All The Shah's Men* (2008).

Kobach, Kris. The Referendum: Direct Democracy in Switzerland (1993).

Kohn, Hans. Nationalism and Liberty: The Swiss Example (1956).

Lee, Ian B. 'Is There a Cure for Corporate "Psychopathy"?' in *American Business Law Journal* 42, 2005, pp. 65 – 90.

Leonard, E.M. *Early History of English Poor Relief* (1900); 'The Enclosure of Common Fields in the 17th Century' in Carus-Wilson (ed.) *Essays in Economic History* (1962) Vol. II.

Lester Richard A. *Monetary Experiments* (1939, 1970).

Levene, Mark. *Genocide in the Age of the Nation State* (2005, 2008: series ongoing).

Lewis, G.C. Remarks on the Use and Abuse of Some Political Terms (1832).

Linder, Wolf. *Swiss Democracy* (1994).

Little, P. and Smith, D.L. Parliaments and Politics during the Cromwellian Protectorate (2007).

Locke, John. *Second Treatise on Civil Government* (1693) available online.

Maine, Henry. *Popular Government* (1885).

Maitland, F.W. *History of English Law Before Edward I* (1898); *The Constitutional History of England* (1898); *State, Trust and Corporation* (2003), *Letters* (1965); 'The Law of Real Property', 'Trust and Corporation', 'The Corporation Sole', 'The Crown as Corporation', 'The Survival of Ancient Communities', 'The Unincorporated Body', 'Moral Personality and Legal Personality', 'The Body Politic' all in *Collected Papers 1-III* (Liberty Fund, online); Introduction to Gierke's *Political Theories of the Middle Ages* (1987).

Mandelstam, Nadezhda. *Hope Against Hope* (1999); *Hope Abandoned* (2011).

Manent, Pierre. Tocqueville and the Nature of Democracy, (1996).

Manin, Bernard. The Principles of Representative Government (1997).

Mann, Michael. The Dark Side of Democracy: Explaining Ethnic Cleansing (2004).

McCraw, Thomas. Prophets of Regulation (1986).

McPherson, James. A Very Civil War: the Swiss Sonderbund War of 1847 (1993).

McKisack, May. The Parliamentary Representation of the English Boroughs During the Middle Ages (1932).

Mansbridge, Jane. Beyond Adversary Democracy (1981).

Marongiou, Antonio. *Medieval Parliaments* (1968).

Martin, J.B. The Grasshopper in Lombard Street (1892).

Martines, Lauro. *Power and Imagination* (1980).

Mencken, H.L. *Notes on Democracy* (2009).

Michels, Robert. Political Parties: A Sociological Study of the Oligarchical Tendencies of Modern Democracy (1911).

Micklethwait and Woolrich. The Company: A Short History of a Revolutionary Idea (2003).

Mill, J.S. *Principles of Political Economy* (1848); 'Centralisation' (1862); available on the Liberty Fund website. Review of Tocqueville's *Democracy in America* (London Review, October 1835).

Millar, John. An Historical View of the English Government (1787).

Miller, Harry E. Banking Theories in the United States before 1860 (1927, 1972).

Minton, Anna. *Ground Control* (2009).

Mints, Lloyd. Monetary Policy for a Competitive Society (1950).

Montesquieu, Baron de. *De l'Esprit des Lois* (1989, tr. Cohler, Miller & Stone).

Mount, Ferdinand. The New Few: or, a Very British Oligarchy (2012).

Muir, Edwin. The Ballad of Everyman.

Namier, Lewis, Monarchy and the Party System (1952 Romanes Lecture); 'Nationality and Liberty', reprinted in Avenues of History (1952); The Structure Of Politics At The Accession Of George III (1957).

Nichols, 'English Government Borrowing 1660-1688' in *Journal of British Studies*, 10,2 1971.

Oakeshott, Michael. 'The Political Economy of Freedom' in *Rationalism in Politics and Other Essays* (1991); 'The Tower of Babel and 'The Rule of Law' in *On History and Other Essays* (1983, 1999); 'Talking Politics' and 'The Masses in Representative Democracy' in *Rationalism in Politics*, 1991; *On Human Conduct* (1975); *The Vocabulary of a Modern European State* (2008); *What is History? and Other Essays* (2004).

Oborne, Peter. The Triumph of the Political Class (2008).

Oresme, Nicole *De Moneta* (14th C.) available online at Mises.org.

Paget's *Law of Banking* (1922 edition is available online: latest edition, 2010).

Palmer, R.R. *The Age of the Democratic Revolution* (1959); 'Notes on the Use of the Word "Democracy" 1789-1799' in *Political Science Quarterly*, June 1953.

Pasquet, D. The Origin of the House of Commons (1925).

Perkins, John. Confessions of an Economic Hitman (2004).

Phillips, C.A. *Bank Credit* (1920).

Pierson, G.W. Tocqueville in America (1959).

Pirenne, Henri. Early Democracy in the Low Countries (1963).

Pollard, A.F. The Evolution of Parliament (1920).

Post, Gaines. 'Plena Potestas and Consent in Medieval Assemblies' in *Traditio* Vol. 1, (1943).

Pound & Plucknett (eds). Readings On The History And System Of The Common Law, 1927.

Powicke, Maurice. *Medieval England* (1950).

Pratt, Julius W. 'American Business and the Spanish-American War' in *American Imperialism in 1898* (1955).

Radford, R.A. 'The Economic Organisation of a P.O.W. Camp' in *Economica* Nov. 1945.

Ressler, Peter & Mitchell, Monika, *Conversations with Wall Street*, (2011).

Ricardo, David. *Works,* Liberty Fund Complete Edition available online.

Rich, Bruce. 'Exporting Destruction' in Steven Hiatt, ed., *A Game As Old As Empire* (2007).

Richards, R.D. The Early History of Banking in England (1958).

Rieff, Philip. Fellow Teachers: of Culture and Its Second Death (1972).

Robbins, Arthur D. Paradise Lost, Paradise Regained (2012).

Robertson, Dennis. Lectures On Economic Principles (1957).

Robinson, Joan. *Freedom and Necessity* (1970).

Rogers, James Harvey. 'The Absorption of Bank Credit' in *Econometrica* 1, 1933.

Rosanvallon, Pierre. 'The History of the Word "Democracy" in France', *Journal of Democracy*, 1995.

Rousseau. *The Social Contract*, tr. G.D.H. Cole (1955).

Russell, Conrad. The Crisis of Parliaments 1509-1660 (1971).

Sanday, Peggy Reeves. Women at the Center: Life in a Modern Matriarchy (2003).

Schleifer, James T. The Making of Tocqueville's 'Democracy in America' (2000).

Schlichter, Detlev, *Paper Money Collapse* (2011).

Schumpeter, Joseph. History of Economic Analysis (1954).

Scott, Tom. The City-State in Europe (2012).

Scrutton, Thomas Edward. 'General Survey Of The History Of The Law Merchant' in *Select Essays in Anglo-American Legal History vol. 3* [1909]. Available online at Liberty Fund.

Sealy and Hooley. Commercial Law: Text, Cases and Materials (2008).

Sheehan, Sean. Copenhagen (2003).

Simons, Henry C. Economic Policy for a Free Society (1948).

Sintomer, Yves. Petite histoire de l'experimentation democratique (2011).

Skidelsky, R. *John Maynard Keynes* (3 Vol.'s: 1983, 1992, 2000).

Smith, Adam. *Wealth of Nations*. Online edition, Liberty Fund.

Smith, Graham. Democratic Innovations (2009).

Smith, Preserved. *The Reformation* (1920).

Sowell, Thomas. Visions of the Anointed (1995).

Steensland, Brian. The Failed Welfare Revolution: America's Struggle Over Guaranteed Income Policy (2008).

Steinberg, Jonathan. *Why Switzerland* (1996),

Sternberg, Elaine. *Just Business* (1994).

Stigler, George J. 'The Theory of Economic Regulation' in *Bell Journal of Economics and Management* 2, 1971.

Stodder, James. *Reciprocal Exchange Networks* (available online, March 2012).

Sutherland, Keith. *A People's Parliament* (2008).

Sweet, Alec Stone. 'The new Lex Mercatoria and Transnational Governance' in *Journal of European Public Policy* 13:5 August 2006: 627–646.

Takuboku, Ishikawa. *Poems to Eat* tr. Carl Sesar, (1969).

Tanner, J.R. English Constitutional Conflicts of the Seventeenth Century (1928).

Tasswell-Langmead's *Constitutional History* (10th edition, revised Plucknett).

Taylor, James. *Creating Capitalism* (2006).

Thirsk, Joan. Economic Policy and Projects (1978); The Rural Economy of England (1984); (ed.) Agrarian History of England and Wales (2011).

Thomas, Hugh. *The Slave Trade* (1977).

Thorne, W.J. *Banking,* (1948).

Tobin, James. 'Financial Innovation and Deregulation in Perspective', in *Monetary and Economic Studies* (Bank of Japan) Vol 3, Issue 2, Sept 1985.

Tocqueville, Alexis de. *Democracy in France.* The edition by. Nolla (2009) contains texts in French and English and much extra material (Liberty Fund, available online); also 'Democracy in Switzerland' published in 1868 edition of *Democracy in America.*

Usher, Abbott Payson. The Early History of Deposit Banking in Mediterranean Europe (Harvard UP, 1943).

Walras, Léon. Études d'Economie Politique Appliquée (1936).

Weber, Max. The Protestant Ethic and the Spirit of Capitalism (1905, 1930).

Werner, R. New Paradigm in Macroeconomics (2005).

White and Notestein. Source Problems in English History (1915).

Whyte, A.B. Self-Government at the King's Command (1933).

Wicksell, Knut. *Interest and Prices* (1898; English translation 1936); 'The Influence of the Rate of Interest on Prices' (1907) available online.

Wiener, Norbert. Cybernbetics (1961); God and Golem, Inc. (1964).

Wikipedia. A wonder of the world today.

Williams, Richard C. The Cooperative Movement: Globalisation from Below (2007).

Wilson, Charles. Profit and Power (1957); England's Apprenticeship (1965); Economic History and the Historian (1969); Profit and Power (1957).

Zeami. *On the Art of the Noh Drama* (15th C. tr. 1984).

Zetterbaum. M. Tocqueville and the Problem of Democracy (1967).